The Cornucopia Proposals

Achieving the American Dream

Capt. David C. Koch

The Aerospace Trust Press

© copyright 2020
The Aerospace Trust Press
(All Rights Reserved)

Copyright © 2020 by The Aerospace Trust Press

All rights reserved under International and Pan-American Copyright Conventions. No part of this book may be reproduced by any mechanical, photographic or electronic process; nor may it be stored in a retrieval system, transmitted or otherwise copied for public or private use without the written permission of The Aerospace Trust Press.

ISBN 9798572308914

Cover Design: Tyler Koch

Published by
The Aerospace Trust Press
2400 E. Main Street, Ste. 103-195
St. Charles, IL 60174

Cornucopia: *An inexhaustible store. Abundance.*

The earliest reference to a cornucopia is found in

Greek and Roman mythology

that dates back nearly 3,000 years.

The name is derived from Latin, cornu copiae

which translates to "horn of abundance".

The most likely source of the horn of abundance symbol

is a story related to the Greek king of all the gods—Zeus.

Gentle Reader,

This book is dedicated to you and our fellow Americans whose souls are yearning for more peace of mind and happiness in their lives.

If, after you read this book, you find that you can believe in the viability of The Cornucopia Proposals put forth herein, please do your part to make them happen. Remember, if you believe, you're half-way there.

Capt. David C. Koch

The Cornucopia Proposals

It is proposed that:

1. the Congress enact the *American Contribution Act of 2021*.

2. the Act establish the *American Contribution Administration* (ACA).

3. the ACA establish the *American Contribution Corps* (ACC).

4. the Congress establish the *American Contribution Trust Fund* (ACTF).

5. the Congress establish the *American Common Good Fund* (ACGF).

6. the Congress establish the *American Cornucopia Fund* (ACF).

Table of Contents

Preface…………………………………………………………………...1

Introduction……………………………………………………...…………...7

Chapter 1: Were We Are Now………………………………………...9

Chapter 2: How We Got Here……………………………………………...23

Chapter 3: Where We Want to Go……………………………...…...81

Chapter 4: How We're Going to Get There…………...…..………....95

Preface

"We hold these truths to be self-evident, that all men are created equal, that they are endowed by their Creator with certain unalienable Rights, that among these are Life, Liberty and the pursuit of Happiness.—That to secure these rights, Governments are instituted among Men, deriving their just powers from the consent of the governed—That whenever any Form of Government becomes destructive of these ends, it is the Right of the People to alter or to abolish it, and to institute new Government, laying its foundation on such principles and organizing its powers in such form, as to them shall seem most likely to effect their Safety and Happiness."

~ *U.S. Declaration of Independence (July 4, 1776)*

July 4, 2020

As an avowed American patriot, it is my custom to re-read the U.S. Declaration of Independence and Constitution each year on the Fourth of July. This Independence Day 2020, roughly 6-months into the Covid-19 pandemic, I find that the Declaration of Independence takes on new meaning for me and many others. Especially with over 25-million Americans protesting in the streets for their unalienable rights of Life, Liberty and the pursuit of Happiness.

The above-quoted section of the U.S. Declaration of Independence gives Americans the flexibility (Or, is it a mandate?) to modify our form of government when it becomes necessary for our "Safety and Happiness". It also guarantees our unalienable rights of Life, Liberty and the pursuit of Happiness.

I think most of my fellow citizens believe these passages are the essential elements of the U.S. Declaration of Independence. And, most of us consider the declaration of equality and the enumeration of our unalienable rights to be at the very core of American culture.

The Covid-19 pandemic has cast a bright light on the current state of inequality in America. I think all of us would agree that the kind of equality we're experiencing in America today is not what the Founders had in mind. This not only applies to minorities, but to all of us given the vast gulf between the financial situations of the poor, not-so-poor, comfortable, well-off, rich and super-rich.

Of course, the "wealth gap" has been with us for a long time. The nature of that gap has changed like a swinging pendulum. But, a constant has been the inability of the poor on one end of the pendulum's swing to eke out even a sustainable living let alone happiness; and the incredible lifestyles of the super-rich on the other. Those of us who live between those two extremes have experienced relatively comfortable lives even though the nature of those lives has changed with the swinging of the pendulum. And, I would argue that our unalienable rights of Life, Liberty and the pursuit of Happiness have been significantly encroached upon rather than enhanced over the course of America's history.

Opinions vary as to the true meaning of the terms "Unalienable", "Life", "Liberty" and "the pursuit of Happiness" as they are used in the U.S. Declaration of Independence. The interpretations I will use in this book are:

Unalienable: Unable to be denied, taken away from or given away by the possessor.

Life: The right to enjoy a lifestyle that provides physical security, good health and wellbeing.

Liberty: The right to enjoy the opportunity to lead one's life without the intervention of others, including the government, as long as one is not endangering or disadvantaging other citizens.

Pursuit of Happiness: The right to lead a meaningful life and achieve self-actualization.

In this book, we'll explore the status of each of these rights and how we got to where we are today. We'll also identify how we can upgrade and update the experience of these rights. And, we will consider some strategies for securing those upgrades and updates.

I ask that you keep an open mind and an optimistic mindset towards the ideas I present in this book. I believe that if these ideas can be transformed into reality in some form or another, many of the current existential threats to the American Dream can be overcome. The benefits we can derive from the new reality can put America on a path to a future that will make all of us stronger, healthier and happier. And they will significantly enhance the chances for the long-term survival of the human race.

Pessimistic critics of the ideas presented in this book will point out that I am not credentialed in the fields of economics, politics, government or healthcare. Therefore, it may seem strange to you that I think I can come up with solutions to the existential problems facing America without specific formal education and training in these areas. But, that's what I've been trained to do—solve problems.

In addition to my formal training as a problem-solver, my experiences as an entrepreneur and professional pilot have revolved around solving problems in a real-world, sustainable and doable manner. As an entrepreneur, I've learned that to bring a solution into existence you must first be a dreamer, then a planner, then a doer and finally a believer. As a professional pilot, I've learned that the first step in solving problems is to be "situationally aware" (e.g., define the problem).

One of the first skills a pilot learns is how to establish and maintain Situational Awareness. It is defined in aviation terms as *"continually monitoring your environment for relevant information, then integrating this data with your previous knowledge of yourself, your aircraft and your environment to form a comprehensive mental model of your current situation and then using that model to anticipate future events and develop alternate plans of action"*. In this book, I'm going to use this situational-awareness model as a framework for discussing where we are now, how we got here, where we want to go and how we're going to get there.

This is my fourth book. However, my previous books are about the aviation-and-space business—"False Security: The Real Story About Airline Safety", "A Personal Flyers Guide to More Enjoyable Flying" and "Air Travelers Heaven". Consequently, you could conclude that I'm out of my depth with the subjects I'm going to address in *"The Cornucopia Proposals"*. I trust that you'll be able to see the logic of my conclusions even though I'm not a healthcare professional, economist or politician—just a senior citizen who's been maintaining situational awareness and solving problems for quite some time.

I've needed to maintain my Situational Awareness because I've been navigating the U.S. healthcare, economic, civic, and cultural systems for over 73-years. And, if you don't maintain Situational Awareness in those situations, you'll quickly find yourself in deep trouble. I received my initial indoctrination to how we do things in America from my German-French-English extended family in a small, mid-western town in the 1950s and 1960s. The politics of the time were framed by World War II, the Korean War, the Cold War and the Vietnam War.

It was a period of rapid and radical social and economic changes. The economic system I grew up and later operated in was "Stakeholder Capitalism" with an emphasis on individualism and entrepreneurship. The civics I learned in the private and public schools I attended were heavily oriented towards the U.S. Constitution and the rule of law. And, the culture I was steeped in emphasized service to community, honesty, perseverance and sacrifice for the common good.

I have been an avid reader since a very early age. Since then, I've read scores of books and articles, and viewed hundreds of movies and videos, on government, economics, culture, education/training and general history. However, I can only claim credentials in organizational culture change and education/training in addition to my aviation, space and entrepreneurial *bone fides*.

My worldview is also informed by my 22-year flight officer career at United Airlines and my 13-year career as an officer and assault-helicopter pilot in the Army National Guard and Reserves. Although I count myself among the progressive elements of our society, my conservative views are equally prominent in my thinking.

So, please consider the source of the ideas and suggestions I am going to present in this book. I like to think my authority for writing *The Cornucopia Proposals* is derived from my being a senior, well-informed U.S. citizen. You'll have to draw your own conclusions on the accuracy and viability of my deductions.

Capt. David C. Koch
July 4, 2020

INTRODUCTION

"The Chinese use two brush strokes to write the word 'crisis.'
One brush stroke stands for danger; the other for opportunity.
In a crisis, be aware of the danger—but recognize the opportunity."
~ John F. Kennedy
U.S. President (1961-1963)

As I write this book (Summer/Fall 2020), we're well into the Covid-19 pandemic. Due to my age (73) and an underlying medical condition, I've been hunkering down at home trying to avoid the reportedly very-unpleasant experience of contracting the virus.

I'm also endeavoring to evade the Grim Reaper since I still have a lot to do and I'm not ready to check out of my mortal coil just yet. If nothing else, I want to see how America weathers this potentially existential pandemic and rising social unrest. However, if my fate is to "fly west" now, it seems to me that I should present the ideas in this book to my fellow citizens while I can.

For the past few years, up until world air travel virtually stopped in mid-March 2020, I have been working on introducing an innovative air-travel solution for U.S. business travelers. Things were going well right up to the time our target customers stopped flying. I've been a serial aviation/aerospace entrepreneur since 1967. This new venture, AirChicago, is my fifteenth startup.

Like most of my fellow non-essential citizens, I've had a lot of time on my hands since my primary occupation is on hold. So, I've been maintaining a daily research regimen that consists of internet searches, reading a couple of chapters in one non-fiction book and one historical-fiction book, perusing several online newsletters and viewing a few current-event *YouTube* channels.

I've been spending a lot of time trying to figure out how we can survive the pandemic. And, I've been trying to solve some nagging societal and economic problems that have been plaguing America for some time.

My ongoing research into economics has yielded an very timely statement by Nobel-Prize-winning economist Milton Friedman (1912-2006). Friedman is widely quoted as saying, *"Only a crisis—actual or perceived—produces real change. When that crisis occurs, the actions that are taken depend on the ideas that are lying around. That, I believe, is our basic function: to develop alternatives to existing policies, to keep them alive and available until the politically impossible becomes the politically inevitable."*

My hope is that *"The Cornucopia Proposals"* will be among the "ideas that are lying around" when our leaders chart a path out of our current crisis. And, if the current crisis inspires enough readers of this book to take action for the adoption of *"The Cornucopia Proposals"*, I believe we have a very good chance of making them a reality.

"The Cornucopia Proposals" is essentially my report on the research I've done, and the conclusions I've come to, regarding the societal, economic and public-health problems that are currently plaguing America. I believe we must solve these problems in the very near future because they are holding humanity back from realizing its full potential.

In my view, we're going to need the full potential of every American to successfully face the challenges confronting us today and in the future. If we fail to solve these problems, I think humanity's future is in serious doubt.

My basic conclusion at this point is that there are several potential silver linings to the existential crises we are now facing. And, we can come up with solutions that will make life better for EVERY American.

My sincere hope is that by the time you finish this book, you will agree with my ideas and conclusions and that you will share them with your family, friends, neighbors, associates and political representatives. And, that you will encourage our leaders to consider them as they chart a course for America's path to a future were every American is happy.

Chapter 1

<u>Where We Are Now?</u>

*"Americans have always evinced some
distrust of government, but the current
situation has exacerbated this to a degree
that may be unprecedented."*
  ~ Eric Alterman
    American Author ("Lying In State: Why Presidents Lie")

In this chapter, we'll explore my situational-awareness model (see Preface) relative to our Unalienable Rights of Life, Liberty and the pursuit of Happiness. This model is based on contemporary events and the knowledge of economics, business, politics and organizational culture that I've acquired over the past 70+ years.

Here are the highlights of my current situational-awareness model relative to the unalienable rights contained in the U.S. Declaration of Independence:

Unalienable Rights: The Founders stated that our rights of Life, Liberty and the Pursuit of Happiness are unalienable. In other words, they can't be denied, taken away from us or given away by us. However, in my situational-awareness model these rights have, to a significant degree, been diminished.

Some would argue that we have given away these rights through inaction at the ballot box and overall lack of political participation. Others believe that these rights have been purposefully taken from us by the Oligarchs that now rule America. In any event, I think that over 95% of Americans would agree that things "just aren't right" anymore. And, that we need to return to a situation where the resources needed to enjoy our rights of Life, Liberty and the pursuit of Happiness are available to <u>every</u> American.

Life: Most constitutional scholars interpret the Declaration of Independence's "right to Life" as the right to enjoy a lifestyle that provides physical security and health. Based on my experience and calculations, in the U.S. today a lifestyle that will provide the right to Life requires an annual income of around $100,000.

According to U.S. Census data, 95% of Americans make less than $100,000 per year. Clearly, almost all the citizens in the U.S. today are not enjoying the right to Life (physical security and health) bestowed upon them by the Founders. They don't have the money they need to pay for good housing, transportation, communications and food. And, they don't have any, or at least adequate, healthcare because of our antiquated, corrupt, unfair and sometimes cruel healthcare system.

Liberty: My interpretation of the "right to liberty" is that we have the right to lead our lives without the intervention of others (including the government) <u>if we are not endangering or disadvantaging our fellow citizens</u>. This comes down to the laws, regulations and cultural norms by which we live our daily lives. Without these, there would be no civilization let alone an America.

Today, Liberty is experienced by Americans in various ways. Liberty depends on justice, and the justice we receive is now dependent on our ethnicity and social status. Also, our contemporary Liberty is constrained by a plethora of commercial, environmental and safety laws and regulations.

Cultural norms play their part to limit our Liberty. And, the work-life balance that most Americans are currently experiencing is certainly not conducive to the exercise of Liberty. In my opinion, our current experience of Liberty in American needs a serious upgrade.

Pursuit of Happiness: Constitutional scholars think that the Founders equated "pursuit" with "practice" when they included the "Pursuit of Happiness" in our unalienable rights. In other words, they really meant (in modern terms) that we have the right to put the idea of happiness into actual practice through the lifestyles we lead.

In my opinion, modern-day America is not a happy place. A May 2020 survey conducted by NORC at the University of Chicago found that Americans are less happy today than they've been in the last half-century. The survey is based on nearly 50-years of research from the General Social Survey.

The survey found that just 14% of adult U.S. citizens indicated they are very happy in 2020. That's about half of those surveyed in 2018 (31%) who said they were very happy. From 1970 through 2019, at least 29% of respondents to the survey have called themselves very happy. And it should be noted that most of the 2020-survey's interviews were completed before the Black Lives Matter movement took off in America.

It is clear to me that the Founders meant for every American to be happy—*not just 14% of us*. Of course, we can't all be very happy all the time. Life has a way of providing counterpoints to or happiness. And, as we'll see later, happiness depends upon our personal abilities to achieve it and the availability of the resources we need to support the practice of happiness. But, I think you will agree with me that most of us should be experiencing happiness most of the time, not just a privileged few.

My current personal situational-awareness model also includes:

A Broken Government: Anyone who has been paying attention to the performance of the American political system in the past 4 decades has witnessed the decline in that system's ability to deliver on our unalienable rights for most of us. The 5% of the U.S. population that now controls our political process is experiencing, for the most part, the American dream of Life, Liberty and the pursuit of Happiness. Unfortunately, most of the rest of us are not.

In his latest book "The System: Who Rigged It, How We Fix It" Professor Robert Reich (former U.S. Secretary of Labor) does his usual exemplary job of explaining that we now live in an oligarchy rather than in a democracy. An oligarchy is a government that is controlled by a relatively small group of people.

The United States now has 630 billionaires whose wealth totaled nearly $3.4 trillion as of April 2020. The 400 richest Americans (according to Forbes rankings) have as much combined wealth as the least-wealthy 205-million people in our country.

Given the facts that wealth equals power and virtually all our elected officials of both parties are beholden to those who finance their campaigns (the Oligarchs and the corporations they control) is it any wonder that our current policies, laws, regulations and cultural norms heavily favor the wealthy at the expense of the rest of us?

A Broken Healthcare System: Over my lifetime, I have personally experienced the best and the worst of the American healthcare system. As a child, my healthcare was covered by my father's employer-provided health-insurance policy. We hadn't yet heard of "co-pays" and as I recall virtually all our healthcare needs were paid for by the insurance companies if you were lucky enough to work for an employer who provided health insurance.

As a United Airlines pilot (1968-1990), my family and I enjoyed a health-insurance benefit that paid for virtually all our medical, dental and vision-care costs with no out-of-pocket or co-pay expenses. That insurance also ensured the best care available no matter the medical problem. And, I was guaranteed to have those health benefits throughout the rest of my life through my United Airlines Pilot retirement plan.

Unfortunately, in 2006 a federal judge allowed the Oligarchs to destroy that retirement plan with the United Airlines bankruptcy. The result for me and my family was vastly reduced retirement benefits and no health insurance. And, I certainly am not the only American who had this experience. Since the early 1980s, the Oligarchs have systematically dismantled the social safety nets of most Americans.

As a self-employed entrepreneur (1990-2012) I was unable to secure health insurance. During these "no-health-insurance" years I was diagnosed with diabetes that was brought on by inadequate healthcare. At times, my out-of-pocket healthcare costs were a threat to my ability to support my family and myself. And, of course, my diabetes diagnosis locked me into a no-healthcare situation due to a pre-existing condition.

When I turned 65 (2012), I qualified for Medicare with a commercial-insurance supplement. Now, for about $2,000 dollars a year plus reasonable co-pays and out-of-pocket expenses I receive what I believe to be adequate healthcare. However, I live in fear that the Medicare benefits I rely on for my continued existence on this planet may be reduced or eliminated.

Today, out of our current population of approximately 328-million people there are about 44-million of us who have no health insurance, and another 38-million who have inadequate health insurance—a total of 82-million (25% of the population). And, many millions more face the likelihood that they will lose their employer-provided health insurance due to layoffs and terminations caused by the pandemic.

Even if you are fortunate enough to have health insurance, you can't necessarily get world-class healthcare in the U.S. anymore. In terms of cost and outcomes, the U.S. healthcare system now ranks among second-world countries. It is currently number-27 in the world. Americans spend more on healthcare than the citizens of any other country, yet our quality-of-care and life-expectancy rankings are below all other developed countries according to the Organization for Economic Co-operation and Development (OECD).

A Broken Educational System: For the first 6 years of my formal education, I attended a private, Catholic-run elementary school. I discovered when I entered the public-school system at age 11 that my basic private-school education placed me ahead of my peers in the "three Rs" (Read'n, Rite'n and 'Rithmatic). When I graduated from a public high school in 1965, I found that I was well prepared for college and for reaching my career goals in a high-tech, leading-edge industry (aviation). My private-college education at Embry-Riddle Aeronautical University was world class.

All of this very-effective education was affordable for my family and me. I had zero student loans when I started working in the aviation industry as a professional pilot even though my flight training alone cost over $100,000 in today's dollars. The total cost of my education and aviation training were covered by my part-time work, my family and society. This experience was shared by my peers. And, we came from a middle-class community.

There is not enough room in this book to address all the problems facing our education system. A partial list includes: lack of performance, lack of funding, overcrowding, inequalities, favoritism, lack of parental involvement, inadequately trained and motivated teachers, a crumbling infrastructure, a hidebound bureaucracy at all levels and high costs.

In the U.S. today, only about 80% of K-12 students graduate from high school. That dismal result is bad enough, but less than 50% of those who do graduate are adequately prepared to succeed in our modern world. And, the costs to society, students, families and our economy are spiraling out of control. At this point, American college graduates have over $1.4-trillion in student debt.

In the U.S. today, most jobs and career paths do not emphasize recurrent and upgrade retraining. To maintain their proficiency in the knowledge and skills they need to safely fly passengers, airline pilots undergo a more-or-less continuing program of education and training.

The common good would benefit greatly if other American workers and professionals did too. And, when Americans are either forced or choose to change career paths, they are on their own for the most part. Widespread career-change-training programs do not exist in America, let alone the financial support that is needed to make the transition.

A Broken News Media: I was taught that the media is the watchdog of our democracy. It's expected to bark when it notices something that "just isn't right". However, when this many-headed watchdog is owned by a small group of oligarchs, one becomes concerned about the accuracy and veracity of the information that is being fed to the American public.

According to Independent Lens, the trend in U.S. media-ownership concentration has been steadily progressing since the shift from stakeholder-capitalism to shareholder-capitalism began in earnest in the early 1980s. Fifty corporations controlled virtually all of the media in the U.S. in 1983. That included magazines, books, music, news feeds, newspapers, movies, radio and television.

That was bad enough, but by 1992, only 25 corporations controlled the American media. It was down to 6 by 2000 and today just 5 dominate the industry—AT&T, Comcast, Disney, ViacomCBS and Fox. With this kind of consolidation of power into the hands of a few oligarchs, is it any wonder the major news outlets can get away with putting out basically 2 "flavors" of "the truth". And, is it any wonder that these 2 flavors are designed to radically polarize Americans?

Ben Bagdikian (Pulitzer-prize winning journalist, former Dean of the Graduate School of Journalism at UC Berkeley and author of The New Media Monopoly) describes the 5 media giants as a "cartel that wields enough influence to change U.S. politics and define social values". And, this cartel is also now consolidating online media under its control.

As a professional communicator, I have been studying the art and science of propaganda for many years. It is obvious to me that the media cartel, which is part of the American Oligarchy, is using standard propaganda techniques on the American public to create a stark divisiveness in the citizenry. We all know the age-old rule for controlling the masses—*divide and conquer*. This strategy has been used by monarchs, oligarchs and tyrants for millennia.

For the past 5 years, Americans have been exposed to the "fake news" phenomenon. In most cases, "fake news" is just an epithet that extreme-right demagogues hurl at the media outlets that lean to the left. This is nothing new. The Soviets first deployed fake news and the claim of fake news early in the last century. They have been perfecting it ever since. Now, in America claims of fake news have bifurcated "truth", making it virtually impossible for one-half of America to agree with the other.

A Broken Economic System: Some would say that the American economic system is rapidly collapsing due to the crisis created by the Covid-19 pandemic. Others argue that it is still OK, but it is on the verge of collapsing. And, still others think that it has been collapsing for at least the past 40 years in terms of how it under-serves over 95% of the American population.

Economic scholars define an economic collapse as "a breakdown of a national economy that typically follows a time of crisis". An economic collapse generally begins at the onset of a severe economic contraction, recession or depression. It can last for a long time depending on the severity of the collapse and the circumstances surrounding the recovery.

The economic collapse that is happening now, or is about to happen, was precipitated by the Covid-19 pandemic. In the early stages of the pandemic, the U.S. Government sent a relief check for $1,200 to approximately 130-million Americans. On July 16, 2020, the U.S. Labor Department reported that 32-million Americans were receiving some form of unemployment benefits.

By the fall of 2020, federal unemployment assistance had dried up because the Republicans in the Senate, led by Mitch McConnell, blocked any further meaningful help to the estimated 50-million Americans who were out of work at that time. It may seem illogical that McConnell would do such a cruel thing to millions of Americans until you realize who he works for (the Oligarchs).

Economic inequality is another hallmark of America's economy today. The structure of the current U.S. capitalist economy ensures that the top 1% of Americans control most of the income and wealth that the economy generates. The U.S. wealth gap refers to the unequal dissemination of assets. These assets include: savings, investments, homes, vehicles, personal valuables, businesses, etc. In 2018, U.S. households held over $113-trillion in assets. As of Q3 2019, the bottom 50% of households held $1.7-trillion (1.6%) of the net worth, and the top 10% held $75-trillion (70%).

According to the Pew Research Center's February 7, 2020 *Fact Tank,* "Over the past 50 years, the highest-earning 20% of U.S. households have steadily brought in a larger share of the country's total income. In 2018, households in the top 20% of earners (with incomes of $130,001 or more that year) brought in 52% of all U.S. income, more than the lower 80% combined, according to Census Bureau data."

Less than 100-years ago, economic mobility was broadly distributed among most Americans although significant disparities remained across demographic groups. Incomes were increasing and parents could reasonably expect a better life for their children. Today, income, wealth and earnings inequality are rising, economic mobility is declining and demographic disparities persist.

Taxes have been the primary means for funding governments since time immemorial. In addition to funding government operations, tax laws have been used to influence behavior. If taxes are fair for all citizens, harmony and optimism are much more likely. If they aren't, discord and pessimism reign. The contemporary American tax system is blatantly weighted in favor of the 5% at the top of the economy while the 95% of Americans who make less than $100,000 per year are unfairly burdened.

Broken Culture: When I was growing up (1947 – 1965), the dominant characteristics of the American culture were service to country, cooperation, compromise and faith in the future. There wasn't a whole lot of difference between the Democrat and Republican Parties and America seemed like a kinder place to live. Most of our society's big decisions were based on science and logic. And, if someone held different political views, you could still maintain a personal or working relationship with them. Not so now.

Today, America's culture is highly polarized. Political compromise at the state and federal levels is rare and becoming rarer. Since the Oligarchs control virtually all our politicians, badly-needed social changes are many times thwarted by one of the 2 parties if the Oligarchs disapprove of the changes. There are distinct differences between the 2 political parties and, to me at least, America has become a dog-eat-dog culture with little-to-no regard for those who need a helping hand up. And, we are witnessing every day the negative results of science denial and irrational decision making.

Contemporary American culture varies considerably from state-to-state and region-to-region. And, there are many subcultures. However, a common denominator is an emphasis on personal freedoms and beliefs. Everyone believes they have the right to loudly, and sometimes violently, voice their opinions. Dissent has become weaponized. Half of Americans believe in the sanctity of individuality and the other half place the common good before individualism.

An attractive social image seems to be a top priority for most Americans, especially those under fifty. In their social media postings, they strive to make their lives appear to be better than they are. At the same time, a large part of the population believes in "keeping it real". However, friendliness and helpfulness are still highly valued.

Economic success, rather than contributing to the common good, has become the goal for most Americans. Traditionalism is no longer honored. Novelty is now what is sought after. The latest trends are followed closely. People want to adopt whatever is currently "cool". Competition for being first is the hottest trend in social media. Higher education has become a status symbol because of its high cost and relative unavailability.

Broken Climate: Science deniers, irrational thinkers and Luddites have been holding sway in politics and economic thinking for the past 4 years. President Trump has withdrawn America from the Paris Climate Agreement and throughout his term in office his appointees gutted the environmental-protection laws, regulations and policies that were put in place by a more-rational national leadership.

I don't think there is a lucid thinker in America today who does not agree that climate change is an existential threat to America and, in fact, the entire human race. Unfortunately, as I write this (Fall 2020), America has chosen to reverse course away from a sustainable future on a habitable planet to what appears to be a straight course into extinction. President-elect Joe Biden has promised to bring America back into the Paris Agreement on his first day in office and to focus on a rapid transition to clean energy.

Broken Infrastructure: To function, the $22-trillion U.S. economy needs a vast infrastructure of airports, freight-and-passenger rail lines, sea ports, roads, bridges, electrical grids, sanitation systems and communications networks. Most of the current American infrastructure was built decades ago. Infrastructure experts and economists believe that delays in upgrading our infrastructure and rising maintenance costs are degrading American economic performance.

Civil engineers are raising safety concerns too. They report that many bridges are structurally unsound and outdated drinking-water and waste-water systems pose public health risks. In many parts of rural America, homes still have septic systems instead of being connected to a local sewage-treatment system.

It was recently discovered that faulty septic systems in poverty-stricken rural Alabama are causing a resurgence in hookworm infections. One in three people sampled in these areas tested positive for traces of hookworm. This gastrointestinal parasite was thought to have been eradicated from the U.S. years ago. Scientists are asking how the richest nation on the planet can accept this poverty-related illness that is at levels comparable to the world's poorest counties.

Meanwhile, other advanced countries enjoy more efficient and reliable services because they have been keeping up with their infrastructure. The U.S. lags other developed countries in infrastructure spending. Experts say that U.S. infrastructure is dangerously overstretched, with a funding gap of more than $2-trillion needed by 2025. President Trump and Republican lawmakers promised several times to come up with an infrastructure-improvement plan, but nothing happened. President-elect Joe Biden has promised to make our national infrastructure a priority.

Most Americans are surprised when they discover that America is not at the top of the list of countries with broadband-internet service. A 2018 *FCC International Broadband Data Report* showed that U.S. broadband speeds ranked number 10 among developed nations. This is just ahead of Norway and Finland. When it comes to pricing, the U.S. ranks 18th out of 23 countries in fixed broadband pricing. And, over 19-million Americans (6% of the population) don't have access to fixed, high-speed internet service. In rural areas, nearly 25% of the population lacks access to the internet.

Broken Work: The Covid-19 pandemic and its economic fallout have put millions of Americans out of work with little-to-no hope of returning to work soon. The continuing rapid development of artificial intelligence, robotics and automation will continue to displace a large percentage of America's workforce from the jobs they now hold. A mid-2020 report indicates that approximately 67% of American businesses are accelerating their pace of automating due to the pandemic.

The nature of work is changing rapidly from being based on the mastery of physical skills to relying on acquiring knowledge-acquisition-and-manipulation capabilities. This change is happening while our educational-and-training systems are bogged down in tradition and bureaucracy.

And, Americans seem to be deluding themselves when they compare the American work experience with that of other developed countries. A 2020 "Second Thought" YouTube video titled "America Compared: Why Other Countries Treat Their People So Much Better" tells the story. The video points out that compensation for low-skilled jobs is much higher in other developed countries.

For example, if you're flipping burgers for McDonalds in the U.S. you will be paid an average of $9 per hour with no benefits. For the same job in Europe, you can earn $27 per hour plus family leave, a generous vacation, paid sick days and a retirement plan. This is true across the board for other low-skilled jobs in America and Europe.

Workers in other developed countries don't have to work 2 jobs to make ends meet as they do in America. And, it doesn't take 2 incomes to support the typical European household like it does here. Unlike in America, a good work-life balance is more reality than dream in other developed countries.

In America, 40-hours per week is considered full time, and full-time jobs typically come with benefits like health insurance, paid sick leave and vacation time. However, in keeping with America's exploitive labor practices American businesses are increasingly giving workers somewhat less than 40-hours per week and re-categorizing them as part-time or "gig" workers—*with no benefits!* And, as gig workers they must pay their FICA and withholding taxes themselves.

Companies like Best Buy, Target and Pets Smart have become notorious for this practice. And, after a $200-million advertising-and-lobbying campaign paid for mostly by Uber and Lyft, California voters just passed a ballot measure that allows companies like Uber and Lyft to classify workers as "gig workers" with no benefits. This was a huge win for gig-economy companies.

By allowing employers rather than the government to define full-time work, American workers are held captive by corporations in a modern form of slavery. They're forced to work ridiculously-long hours to qualify for benefits, or they have to work at least 2 jobs to be able to feed their families and afford healthcare. Both options lead to a terrible work-life balance.

American workers are forced to endure a work-life balance that workers in other developed countries find deplorable. At the same time, real wages have fallen and benefits have shrunk for American workers.

Over the past 3 decades, American workers have developed an unhealthy work-life balance. For example, in 1960 only 20% of American women worked. Today, in 70% of households with children both adults work full time. In 2019, over 85% of men and 66% of women worked more than 40-hours per week. Americans work 137 more hours per year than Japanese workers, 260 more hours than British workers and 499 more hours per year than French workers.

When it comes to vacation time, American workers are far worse off than their counterparts in other developed countries. In almost every developed country except America, employers are required to provide paid-vacation and sick days and employers are mandated to pay employees fairly. And, workers in other industrialized countries get more paid vacation and sick days than U.S. workers.

Paid parental leave is another area where American workers have fallen distantly behind workers in other advanced countries. Most work experts believe that paid parental leave is essential to a good work-life balance and it benefits employers because workers are happier and less stressed.

But, the most important long-term benefit is, of course, realized by parents and children. With adequate paid parental leave, parents and children bond more effectively. This leads to a healthier and saner next generation. Due to American businesses' obsession with the bottom line, America is the only industrialized nation on the planet that does not mandate at least some paid parental leave.

Clearly, America is not living up to its claim of being the greatest nation on Earth. It consistently ranks near-to-or-at dead last in terms of work metrics. Why is it that the most-wealthy nation on Earth can't pay its workers a fair wage and provide them with health insurance, paid sick leave, paid parental leave and adequate paid-vacation time. In my opinion, it's not a matter of "can't" but a matter of "won't". American business people worship the almighty dollar. Profit is king and the peasants struggle to survive.

In summary, my assessment of the current situation has me alarmed. With millions of people in the streets of America demanding more-equal rights and an oligarchy that appears to be committed to divisiveness, conflict and a total disregard for our unalienable rights, I fear that things can easily get out of hand. And that could set our country back literally hundreds of years while casting most of us in America into poverty with its consequent misery.

As a member of the Illinois Army National Guard, I served on the streets of Chicago during the riots in the late 1960s. Although "America was burning" then, I did not feel so close to anarchy and tyranny as I do now. I believe that if chaos ensues, our unalienable rights will be but a dim memory. I pray that rational and compassionate heads prevail, not the forces of evil that are attempting to run roughshod over Americans today.

Chapter 2

How We Got Here

"Those who do not remember the past are condemned to repeat it.".
~ George Santayana
Philosopher (1863 – 1952)

If we wish to establish and maintain situational awareness, we must know how we got to where we are. So, let's look at a brief history of the American experience as it relates to where we are and where we want to go.

Unalienable Rights: The Founders told us through their writings that the rights enumerated in the U.S. Declaration of Independence—Life, Liberty and the pursuit of Happiness—are unalienable. They can't be denied, taken away from us or given away by us. The U.S. Declaration of Independence tells us that these rights were given to all humans by their creator, and that governments are created to protect them.

The Declaration of Independence was drafted by Thomas Jefferson, and it was edited by the Committee of Five that consisted of Jefferson, John Adams, Benjamin Franklin, Roger Sherman and Robert Livingston. It was further edited and adopted by the Committee of the Whole of the Second Continental Congress on July 4, 1776. The second paragraph of the first article in the Declaration of Independence contains the phrase "Life, Liberty and the pursuit of Happiness".

John Locke, an English philosopher and physician (1632 – 1704), had a significant influence on the Founding Fathers' thinking about human rights. According to Locke, the legitimate basis of government is to protect the unalienable natural rights that everyone has had bestowed upon them by simply being born a human.

Over the 224 years since the U.S. Declaration of Independence was first published, the unalienable rights given to us by the Founders have been available to Americans in varying degrees depending upon the times and an individual's standing in society. Those who have been among America's top 5% (in terms of income and wealth) have had the means and opportunity to enjoy Life, Liberty and the Pursuit of Happiness. Unfortunately, most of the rest of us have not. And, the Americans at the bottom of the socio-economic ladder have had their unalienable rights systematically withheld from them from the founding of the country to today.

Life: Life expectancy is one metric for quality of life. In 2020, an average American can expect to live 79 years. In 1950, it was 68. At the time of the Declaration of Independence (1776) it was only 38. The average life expectancy has increased by 41-years since the United States of America was founded. However, the life expectancy for non-white and poor Americans is considerably lower due to the unavailability to them of adequate healthcare, a healthy diet and the other problems associated with being poor.

In order to enjoy a decent life, one must have enough money to pay for it. It appears to me that over 95% of Americans don't have the means to secure the resources that are critical to a decent lifestyle—good housing, adequate nutrition, healthcare, personal safety, etc. This has been the case since America was founded and it persists today.

Liberty: Most Americans equate "liberty" with "freedom". They believe that liberty is the ability to do as one pleases. However, liberty requires the responsible exercise of freedom under the rule of law while not depriving others of their freedom.

America's history has had its highs and lows in ensuring liberty for its citizens. The Founding Fathers set high standards for our new nation to live up to when they wrote the Declaration of Independence in 1776. However, since then the debate about the best way to meet these standards has been an integral part of the American experiment.

In the earliest years of our new nation, many people thought the U.S. Constitution gave the federal government too much power over its people. The first 10 amendments to the Constitution were ratified in December 1791 as the "Bill of Rights". It guaranteed certain fundamental rights that included freedom of speech and religion, the right to bear arms and the right to a fair trial. The Bill of Rights greatly expanded the civil liberties of Americans. Its implications are still being debated today.

The absence of the prohibition of slavery in the Constitution is one of the great paradoxes of our founding era. The Framers were revolutionary thinkers who created what would become the first successfully functioning government "by the people". Their ideas of fairness, justice, and individual rights are what most Americans believe in today. Why, did so many brilliant minds pledge to be champions of individual rights on the one hand and allow human beings to be reduced to chattel on the other?

The answer may lie in the idea of compromise. The Founders apparently compromised their morals and power in the name of economics and to ensure the Constitution would be ratified. Slavery, when all was said and done, was both profitable and convenient for many white Americans—and not just in the South.

President Abraham Lincoln had become convinced by 1862 that the South's slaves had to be freed if there was any chance of winning the Civil War and maintaining the Union. He signed the Emancipation Proclamation in that year and it took effect in 1863. In his Gettysburg Address, Lincoln made in clear that the North was now fighting for a "new birth of freedom" while endeavoring to keep America unified.

In 1865 (89-years after the Declaration of Impendence was issued), the passage of the 13th Amendment to the U.S. Constitution abolished the institution of slavery in the United States. The Amendment granted liberty to more than 4-million black men, women and children formerly held in bondage.

Between 1880 and 1920, over 20-million immigrants came to America in pursuit of liberty, safety and happiness. The Eastern Europeans and Jews were fleeing religious persecution, the Italians were fleeing hunger and poverty and the Armenians and Mexicans were escaping from war or revolution at home. America welcomed these new arrivals. This open-door policy ended with the onset of World War I (1914 – 1918). In the 1920s, a series of new laws were introduced to limit immigration.

In 1920, after 72-years of epic struggle, the 19th Amendment was ratified. It gave women the right to vote. Before the Amendment was ratified, women protestors went on hunger strikes and they were arrested and imprisoned. After the last state (Tennessee) ratified the Amendment in August 1920, women across America flocked to the polls in the fall to vote for a new president.

In 1963, after years of unrest and setbacks, advocates for equal liberty celebrated the passage of sweeping legislation that prohibited racial discrimination. The Civil Rights Act was introduced by President John F. Kennedy and championed after Kennedy's assassination by

President Lyndon B. Johnson. Johnson doggedly pushed the bill through Congress despite stiff opposition from the Democrats. On June 2, 1964, Johnson signed into law the Civil Rights Act, which ended the segregation of public and many private facilities. It also outlawed discrimination based on race, color, religion, sex or national origin.

The Supreme Court issued a landmark ruling in 2015 that declared that the Constitution guarantees same-sex couples the freedom to marry. The decision echoed the Court's 1967 verdict in *Loving v. Virginia* which struck down state laws banning interracial marriage. Justice Anthony Kennedy declared that the freedom to marry was one of the most fundamental liberties guaranteed to individuals under the 14th Amendment, and should apply to same-sex couples just as it does to heterosexual couples. "They ask for equal dignity in the eyes of the law," Kennedy wrote. "The Constitution grants them that right."

So, we can see that Liberty (Freedom) has had a rather spotty history in America. Another complicating factor in the history of Liberty in the U.S. is the fact that Liberty is in the eye of the beholder. Many believe that Liberty gives them the license to do as they please no matter the consequences to themselves and/or to the common good. Others think that Liberty must be tempered by laws, regulations and norms that take the liberty, security and safety of others into account.

Happiness: As we saw in Chapter 1, for the past 50-years only about one-third of Americans have considered themselves to be "very happy". I think it is safe to assume that before 1970, the percentage of people who were "very happy" was even lower. And now, just 14% of adult Americans are "very happy". With the effects of the pandemic likely to still be with us in 2021, it is highly probable that even fewer American's will self-identify as "very happy".

In her excellent 2015 article *A Brief History of Happiness: How America Lost Track of the Good Life—and Where to Find It Now*, *Yes! Magazine* editor Sarah Van Gelder points out, "For decades, we've been taught that economic growth and buying more stuff will make us happy while trashing the planet. The good news is that there's a better kind of happy. It starts with meaningful work, loving relationships and a thriving natural world."

In the 1940s, Abraham Maslow (American psychologist 1908 – 1970) put forth his <u>Maslow's Hierarchy of Human Needs</u>. In the decades since then, an untold number of psychologist, behaviorists and social scientist have expressed their alignment with Maslow's thinking. Most agree that if one achieves the pinnacle of Maslow's hierarchy (it's usually portrayed graphically as a pyramid), one can achieve happiness.

Unfortunately, in my opinion not nearly enough attention has been paid to the efficacy of Maslow's Hierarchy when social, political and economic decisions have been made. This is so even though Maslow's Hierarchy is generally believed to be a roadmap to happiness.

I believe that the shareholder capitalism that has held sway since the 1970s is largely to blame for this critical oversight. When priority is given to the happiness of the few (shareholders) over the happiness of the many (workers, customers, professionals, etc.), the resources needed to climb Maslow's Pyramid are thereby diverted to make the rich happy at the expense of everyone else's happiness.

Government: America's Founders started us out on the right track by declaring that "all men are created equal" and "That to secure these rights, Governments are instituted among Men, deriving their just powers from the consent of the governed." Unfortunately, in America today our government is not living up to what the Founders had in mind.

We got to this undesirable condition over the past 40-years or so by way of a strategy that was conceived by elite capitalists. That strategy included shareholder capitalism (Milton Friedman in the 1970s) and the addiction of politicians to campaign contributions provided to them by those elites.

The strategy also included the U.S. Supreme Court's decision in the Citizens United case in 2010. This decision enabled the complete corruption of national politics that has resulted in control of our government by the New Oligarchs. These oligarchs now obviously have the power to decide our tax laws as well as our social programs (or lack thereof). As a result, the Oligarchs and their corporations pay little-to-no U.S. taxes and they are in the process of shredding our social safety net.

Inequality has become systemic. And the gutting of environmental and safety regulations has been both quick and thorough over the past 4 years. The rich get richer, and the poor get poorer, and our current government seems hell-bent on hastening rather than curbing climate change. It became much harder for the American people to express their will at the ballot box with the gutting of the Voter's Rights Act in 2013.

Healthcare: The history of organized healthcare in America has been significantly different from most other developed countries. Healthcare was rudimentary when the Declaration of Independence was sent to King George III. Mortality was very high in those early days. There was no government regulation or much attention paid to public health.

The first medical society in America was established in 1735. In 1750, the first hospital in America was built. The Medical College of Philadelphia was founded in 1765. The medical department of King's College was established 1770. The first medical degrees were awarded in the 1770s. In 1836, the Library of the Surgeon General's Office was established when Joseph Lovell, then Surgeon General, purchased reference books and journals for his office. In 1840, the library published its first list of publications.

In the American Civil War (1861 – 1865), more soldiers died of disease than from fighting. However, the war excited a wave of progress in medical-and-healthcare research, surgical techniques, nursing and healthcare facilities. There were U.S. Army hospitals in every state.

Healthcare activists of the era brought significant improvements to America's budding healthcare system. This progress was supported by the United States Sanitary Commission and the United States Army Medical Department. Other government health-related agencies were established during this time. The states also initiated healthcare programs.

The American Medical Association (AMA) was founded in 1849. By 1899, it had grown its membership to nearly half the physicians in America. Most healthcare up to this point in time was provided as a "fee-for-service" with payment due at the time of care. Some private insurance pools and employer-provided healthcare existed. The U.S. Army established the Hospital Corps in 1886.

The President at the turn of the century, Theodore Roosevelt (1901-1909), made health insurance a priority for his administration. He famously said, "No country can be strong whose people are sick and poor." However, most of the healthcare initiatives in the early 1900's were led by non-governmental organizations.

The industrial revolution of that time required most workers to work in a dangerous environment. Workplace injuries increased rapidly. Fortunately, unions were gaining traction. They negotiated contracts with the employers that shielded union members from disastrous financial losses due to workplace injury or illness. Companies began to provide various forms of health insurance.

Concurrently, the Progressive Party was pushing the idea of a National Health Service and public healthcare for the unemployed, elderly and disabled. The AMA and other organizations put up strong opposition to the plan, and the American working class wasn't supportive of the idea of compulsory healthcare. In 1916, the Progressive Party dissolved, thereby ensuring that the U.S. wouldn't experience the groundswell of public support for public healthcare that leading European nations would experience soon after.

After the start of World War I in 1914, Congress enacted the War Risk Insurance Act. The Act covered military personnel and their dependents in the event of death or injury. The War Risk Insurance program essentially ended with the conclusion of the war in 1918, though benefits continued to be paid to survivors and their families.

Following the war, healthcare costs rose beyond the reach of most Americans. In 1923, a Texas hospital created what was probably the country's first private-healthcare program. The hospital worked with local schools to provide healthcare to teachers for a monthly premium. The program rapidly expanded across America. The program evolved into the non-profit Blue Cross/Blue Shield insurance company. Other new private-health-insurance enterprises soon followed.

With the onset of the Great Depression in in the early 1930s, healthcare for all Americans became a top priority. Especially for the elderly and the unemployed. President Franklin D. Roosevelt (1933 – 1945) backed the idea of universal healthcare by championing a health-insurance bill. Unfortunately, the American Medical Association and others vigorously opposed it and it was never passed.

In 1933, Henry Kaiser, who was leading the effort to build the Grand Coulee Dam, contracted with private doctors to provide healthcare for his 6,000+ employees working on the world's largest construction project. Other construction projects adopted this approach to employee healthcare.

Shortly after the U.S. entered World War II at the end of 1941, Congress passed the Stabilization Act of 1942. The Act prohibited business from paying higher wages. So, American companies turned to other employee recruitment-and-retention enticements like employer-paid health insurance. Most healthcare historians mark this as the beginning of the employer-provided health insurance programs we still have today.

America's entry into World War II required a rapid expansion of the Henry Kaiser Shipyards. Kaiser once again contracted with private doctors to provide a pre-paid group practice for these shipyard workers. This program eventually became the Kaiser Permanente Health Plan. It developed into our present-day managed-care system of HMOs and PPOs.

After the war, employers continued to use employer-paid health insurance as a recruitment tool. They were intent on recruiting the best workers available from the pool of returning veterans. However, employer-paid health insurance did not solve the healthcare problem for many Americans who were unemployed, retired or disabled. Also, there were still many employers who did not provide this benefit.

There were many efforts over the ensuing years to solve this problem of unequal healthcare. In 1943, the Wagner-Murray-Dingell Bill was introduced. It proposed universal healthcare funded through a payroll tax. Due to opposition from the American Medical Association (AMA), the private-insurance companies and other ideologues, the bill never made it out of committee.

President Harry Truman (1945 – 1953) took up the cause for universal healthcare early in his first term, but his best efforts were met with skepticism in Congress. They called his plan "socialist" and claimed that it was communistic in nature. Truman's universal-healthcare plan died a slow death during his second term as public support dwindled due to aggressive propaganda campaigns by the AMA and the private-insurance companies.

As the idea of universal healthcare lost its luster, citizens without employer-provided health insurance began purchasing private-health-care plans if they could afford to do so. During this time, labor unions used employer-paid healthcare as a bargaining chip during contract negotiations. And, it became obvious to employers they could use employer-paid healthcare as a way to keep employees in bondage to the employer.

By 1960, national expenditures for healthcare amounted to 5% of U.S. GDP. Early in his first term, President John F. Kennedy (1961-1963) tried once again to introduce a healthcare plan for senior citizens. He promoted his plan by encouraging Americans to get involved in the legislative process and he put pressure on Congress to pass the bill. However, due to opposition by the AMA, private-insurance companies and anti-socialist political activists the bill failed.

Vice President Lyndon B. Johnson (1963-1969) became President after Kennedy was assassinated in 1963. He continued the fight for a government health plan for senior citizens. Johnson's proposal included an expansion of the Social Security Act of 1935 and grants to hospitals in need of modernization if they would provide medical services to those who could not afford them. After numerous amendments to Johnson's bill, Congress passed it. Because of the Congressional changes, opposition to the bill was tepid. The bill was the precedent for Medicare and Medicaid.

The national healthcare bill had climbed to almost 7% of GDP by the time Richard Nixon was elected to the presidency in 1968. This was partially due to Medicare expenses. Nixon, although he was a Republican, proposed new national-healthcare legislation. And, in 1971 Senator Edward Kennedy introduced a single-payer plan. Other members of Congress were also working on a similar plan.

Nixon's plan required employers to offer health insurance to employees. He offered employers subsidies to help them offset the cost of the plan. Nixon believed in the open marketplace and he thought that making the public healthcare program part of it was the best way to go.

The plan would have covered almost all Americans—those with jobs (and their families) would get their healthcare insurance through their employers and when they retired they'd be covered by Medicare. Nixon thought the bill would fly with the AMA, the private-health-insurance companies and the far-right ideologues. Advocacy for the plan broke down with a disagreement between President Nixon and Senator Kennedy. After negotiations failed, the Watergate scandal grabbed national attention, and support for any new healthcare plan evaporated.

However, before he resigned, Nixon made progress on 2 healthcare-related fronts. Congress passed, and Nixon signed into law, the Social Security Act Amendment of 1972 and the Health Maintenance Organization Act of 1973. This legislation brought some order to the healthcare industry.

By the 1980s, the national cost of healthcare had risen to almost 9% of GDP. President Reagan (1981-1989) watered down federal-healthcare regulations, and he encouraged the privatization of the healthcare system (as well as most other industries). However, during Reagan's tenure the Consolidated Omnibus Budget Reconciliation Act of 1986 (COBRA) was passed into law. It allowed separated employees to maintain their previous employers group health-insurance plan. But, they had to pay relatively high premiums for the coverage.

In the 1990s, national-healthcare costs climbed to 12% of GDP. President Bill Clinton (1993-2001) proclaimed these rapidly increasing costs would be a drag on the economy and it would hurt average Americans. Clinton proposed the Health Security Act of 1993. The Act was like Franklin D. Roosevelt's and Nixon's plans. It included universal healthcare coverage and it protected the private-health-insurance system that had evolved in the absence of national-healthcare legislation.

By the end of 1993, there was still no consensus regarding the legislation and the bill quietly died without even being put to a vote. The shift from stakeholder capitalism to shareholder capitalism was well underway by this time. The Oligarchs were increasingly having their way with the American government and economy. They opposed the legislation.

But, Clinton made some progress towards a national-healthcare program when he signed the Health Insurance Portability and Accountability Act (HIPAA) in 1996. The Act mandated privacy standards and guaranteed that individual medical records were available to patients. It also placed restrictions on how group-health plans treated pre-existing conditions. Clinton was also able to include the Children's Health Insurance Program (CHIP) in the Balanced Budget Act of 1997. It expanded Medicaid to certain uninsured children. CHIP is run by the states, and it is still in use today.

As part of the swing of the capitalism pendulum from stakeholder capitalism to shareholder capitalism, employers were rapidly finding ways to reduce their employee-health-insurance costs. And, insurance companies were trying to gain more control over how healthcare was provided.

By 2000, the National Healthcare Expense accounted for over 13% of GDP. President George W. Bush (2001-2009) wanted to update Medicare to include prescription drug coverage. The Medicare Prescription Drug, Improvement and Modernization Act of 2003 (Part D) was signed into law. Enrollment was optional, but millions of Americans are still benefiting from it.

President Barack Obama (2009-2017) wasted no time getting to work on healthcare reform once he took office. He and Senator Ted Kennedy created a new healthcare law that was similar to the one Ted Kennedy and Nixon worked on in the 1970s. The plan mandated that most large employers provide health insurance to their employees. It also required all Americans to have health insurance even if their employer did not offer it. The proposed bill would use an "open marketplace" in which private-insurance companies could not deny coverage to Americans with pre-existing conditions. If an American citizen earned less than 400% of the poverty level, he/she could qualify for subsidies to help cover the cost of the insurance premiums.

President Obama steered away from a universal healthcare (single-payer) approach because it was opposed by the Oligarchs. Instead, the proposal was based on using the existing private-health-insurance model to extend health-insurance coverage to millions of Americans. After a massive struggle with Congress, President Obama signed the Patient Protection and Affordable Care Act (PPACA) in 2010. The new law was the most-significant overhaul and expansion of healthcare coverage in the U.S. since the passage of Medicare and Medicaid in 1965.

Eight-million Americans took advantage of the Affordable Care Act Marketplace during the first open enrollment season. Over 12-million Americans have enrolled in the program to-date. However, the Republicans have put unrelenting pressure on the Act because it *requires* employers to provide health-insurance coverage for their employees. Those who oppose the bill often trot out the time-worn socialism bogyman. The Republicans are also challenging some provisions of the Act in the U.S. Supreme Court. To-date Republicans in Congress have forced over 50 votes on repealing the Affordable Care Act—*all without success.*

For the past 4-years, President Donald Trump has been trying to gut not only Social Security but also the Affordable Care Act. He has offered no coherent plan to replace the Affordable Care Act or offered any other form of adequate healthcare coverage to Americans even though 87-million (45%) of American adults aged 19-to-64 do not have adequate health insurance. Notwithstanding the Republican campaign to destroy it, the ACA has proven to be remarkably resilient. The Affordable Care Act has done a extraordinary job of expanding healthcare to more Americans. President-elect Joe Biden has promised to improve and expand the Affordable Care Act when he takes office.

Education: The curricula used in American schools today is quite different from those used in colonial times.

When public education was organized in the U.S. in 1635, most curricula featured religion, family and morality. Schools of the time didn't emphasize academic instruction. Education for girls was very limited.

By the 1850s, academic instruction began to make traction in school curricula around the young country. Literacy was promoted through "Read'n, Right'n and 'Rithmatic" (the 3 Rs). At that point, public-school enrollment was around 59%. Thirty-one states required public-school attendance for American children by 1900. With the demand for public education growing rapidly, by 1918 all 48 states mandated it.

In the 1920s, school districts across the country introduced more academic subjects like English and Social Studies. In the 1950s, public-school attendance rose to almost 75%. Today, it is at 94%.

The Elementary and Secondary Education Act of 1965 (ESEA) was part of President Lyndon Johnson's War on Poverty. The Act moved education to the forefront of the national offensive to eradicate poverty. It was a landmark commitment to equal access to quality education for all American children.

In 2001, President George W. Bush proposed the No Child Left Behind Act (NCLB). It updated the Elementary and Secondary Education Act, and effectively scaled up the federal role in holding schools accountable for student outcomes. The major focus of the NCLB was to close student achievement gaps by providing all children with a fair, equal and significant opportunity to obtain high-quality education.

The NCLB was criticized by many Americans because they believed that it forced teachers to "teach to the test" so that students would do better on standardized tests. The critics asserted that student learning and teacher creativity were stifled by the Act. As a long-time FAA-Certificated ground-and-flight instructor who has fought the "teach to the test" mentality in the aviation world, I agree with those critics.

Critics also charged that the NCLB caused the federal government to intrude too much into state-public-school systems. Also, these critics contended that the NCLB resulted in unfunded federal mandates. This, they claimed, passed associated financial problems from the federal government to the states. Additionally, they argued that the NCLB placed excessive emphasis on teacher qualifications and standardized testing. Another huge problem with the NCLB was that the high-school-graduation rate was going down and the number of students attending college was considerably lower.

The Every Student Succeeds Act (ESSA) was signed by President Obama in 2015. It replaced the 2001 No Child Left Behind Act. When it was put into effect, most Americans considered it to be good news for our nation's schools. The Act retains a role for the federal government in public education, but it places the primary responsibility on the states for establishing educational standards. The ESSA advances equality among students and it requires high standards of learning, further preparing students for college and careers. Unfortunately, today it is estimated that nearly half (47%) of high-school graduates are not prepared for either.

And, of course, the Covid-19 pandemic has wreaked havoc on the American public-school system. Most students are currently experimenting with distance learning and/or hybrid courses (a mix of distance and in-person learning). I have been a proponent of hybrid learning since I started teaching people to fly in 1965. That belief was reinforced recently when I used the technique in a college course I taught. It was a combination of online and in-classroom learning.

News Media: In colonial times, Americans got their local news by word-of-mouth and the printing press. American newspapers began as modest sidelines for printers. The colonies boasted several local newspapers well before the Declaration of Independence was signed. But, it wasn't until 1704 that the first continuous newspaper was launched in Boston. The high literacy rate extant in the city at that time, coupled with the desire for self-government, made Boston the perfect location for this important milestone.

In 1765, the Stamp Tax increased the cost of publishing newspapers. This led to the failure of several newspapers. Even though the Stamp Tax was repealed in 1766, newspaper editors and writers began questioning the right of the British to control the colonies. They were quick to inform Americans of British misdeeds and to encourage a revolt against King George III.

The publication of the *Federalist Papers* and the *Anti-Federalist Papers* in the 1780s, moved the nation into the "party-press era". As is the case today, partisanship dominated early Americans' choice of editorial content. The rise of the party press was caused primarily by the cost of producing and distributing newspapers. The cost could not be covered by subscriptions and advertisements alone. So, political parties stepped in with financial help to support newspapers that sided with them.

Newspapers began circulating partisan party propaganda. Just like today's media, they publicly attacked political leaders of the other party and supported those with the same political agenda. Because of the dominance of the party press at that time, the Founders came to believe that a free press is essential for creating an informed electorate. As we know, freedom of the press is codified in the Bill of Rights (Article 3).

After 1830, manufacturing advancements and new means of transportation enabled newspapers to expand their reach and reduce their costs. New newspapers entered the market and rapidly expanded their readership. Although most of the early content was gossip and fictional accounts, most newspapers expanded their coverage to include sports, the weather and educational pieces.

Before the Civil War (1861 – 1865), few newspaper reporters adhered to high journalistic standards. By the end of the Civil War, professional standards of accuracy and impartiality were spreading throughout the newspaper industry. To entertain as well as to inform, newspapers introduced editorial pages, cartoons and pictures. But, the front pages remained dramatic and shocking. The sensational style of coverage became known as "yellow journalism".

As newspapers became more popular, advertisements generated more-and-more income for the paper. The financial rewards for owning a newspaper increased and competition for circulation and ad revenues heated up. In 1896, the *New York Times* brought the "informational model" back to the newspaper business. This business model focused on important political, economic and world news rather than sensationalism and entertainment. *The New York Times* pioneered transparency, accuracy and impartiality in reporting the news.

The Progressive Era (1890s – 1920s), a time of intense political and social reform targeted at progressing to a better society, ushered in newspaper "muckraking". This flavor of journalism focused on coverage that exposed corrupt government and business practices. Some reporters of the era, like Upton Sinclair, had a great influence on the common good and the treatment of industrial workers by their employers. Prior to the rise of television in the early 20th century, the average American read several newspapers every day.

The consolidation of the newspaper industry in America began in the late 20th century and accelerated in the early 21st century. This consolidation placed ownership of most media properties in the hands of a few large corporations. It also shifted editorial and business decisions to people without a personal stake in the local communities where their papers are located.

In the U.S. today, the top 25 newspaper companies control the fate of nearly 33% of all newspapers. That's up from 20% in 2004. Roughly 50% of all newspapers in America today changed ownership over the past 15-years (some multiple times). Since 2014, most of the 1,200 papers sold have been either family-owned enterprises or small private regional chains. The most active purchasers of newspapers in recent years have been New Media/GateHouse, Adams Publishing and AIM Media. Over the past four years, these 3 chains have purchased nearly a third of the paper companies that were sold.

Virtually all American newspapers now face an existential threat from digital journalism. Their traditional readers are turning to the new media for their news and entertainment, and advertisers are following them.

Radio news made its appearance in America in the 1920s. The National Broadcasting Company (NBC) and the Columbia Broadcasting System (CBS) began running sponsored news programs and radio dramas. Comedy programs, such as *Amos 'n' Andy*, *The Adventures of Gracie*, and *Easy Aces*, became popular during the 1930s, as listeners were trying to find humor and relief during the Depression.

Talk shows, religious shows, and educational programs followed, and by the late 1930s, game shows and quiz shows were added to the airwaves. Approximately 83% of households had a radio by 1940, and most tuned in regularly. The spread of the radio brought timely news and entertainment to rural America as well as to the cities.

As radio listenership grew, politicians realized that the medium offered a cost-effective way to reach the public. President Warren Harding (1921 – 1923) was the first president to regularly give speeches over the radio.

However, it was President Franklin D. Roosevelt (1933 – 1945) who famously harnessed the political power of radio. He delivered his first radio speech 8-days after assuming the presidency. His radio speeches became known as "fireside chats" and provided an important way for him to promote his New Deal agenda. The combination of personal charm, persuasive rhetoric and the radio allowed Roosevelt to expand both the government and the presidency beyond their traditional roles.

The Radio Act of 1927 created the Federal Radio Commission (FRC). It set the first standards for public radio transmissions (frequencies, station licenses, etc.). However, the FRC had little authority. This was resolved in 1934 with the passing of the Communications Act. It shut down the FRC and created the Federal Communications Commission (FCC). The new commission worked with radio stations to assign frequencies and set national standards, as well as oversee other forms of broadcasting. The FCC was also charged with overseeing the new communications medium of the telephone. The FCC still regulates interstate communications.

The conflict in Europe that began in 1939 with the German invasion of Poland changed radio news forever. The subsequent World War II fed a desire for frequent news reports about the constantly evolving war. Newspapers, with their once-a-day printing, were too slow.

To protect wartime military operations, the White House issued guidelines on the reporting of classified information. This constituted a legal exception to the First Amendment's protection against government involvement in the press. Newscasters voluntarily agreed to suppress information about the development of the atomic bomb, military deployments, strategic plans and other sensitive matters.

Broadcast radio enjoyed almost universal listenership well into the late 20th century. However, television and satellite radio have taken a significant market share from traditional radio-broadcast stations. This has been mitigated somewhat by radio stations establishing a presence on the internet.

The introduction and rapid spread of television changed media forever. The first TV broadcast in American covered President Franklin Roosevelt's speech at the opening of the 1939 World's Fair in New York. The public did not immediately start buying televisions, but coverage of World War II changed their minds. CBS-TV reported on war events and included pictures and maps that enhanced the news for viewers. By the 1950s, the price of television sets had dropped, more televisions stations were being built and advertisers were buying up advertising spots.

Predictably, quiz and games shows dominated the television airwaves in its early days. But when the popular World War II radio reporter and commentator Edward R. Murrow made the move from radio to television in 1951, television journalism gained its foothold. As television programming expanded, more channels were added. Networks such as ABC, CBS, and NBC began nightly newscasts, and local stations and affiliates followed suit.

Television enabled politicians to connect with voters even better than radio did. With television, voters could see a president or candidate speak or answer questions in an interview. This gave everyone the opportunity to decode body language and tone to help them to decide whether candidates or politicians were sincere.

The first political advertisements were run on television by presidential candidates Dwight D. Eisenhower and Adlai Stevenson in the early 1950s. They were primarily radio jingles with animation or short question-and-answer sessions. In 1960, John F. Kennedy's campaign used a Hollywood-style approach to promote his image as young and vibrant. The Kennedy campaign ran interesting and engaging ads, featuring Kennedy, his wife Jacqueline and everyday citizens who supported him. Sound familiar?

Television also became useful as a way to combat scandals and accusations of impropriety. Republican vice-presidential candidate Richard Nixon used a televised speech in 1952 to address accusations that he had illegally taken money from a political campaign fund. Nixon laid out his finances, investments and debts and ended by saying that the only election gift the family had received was a cocker spaniel the children named Checkers. The "Checkers speech" is remembered more for humanizing Nixon than for proving he had not taken money from the campaign account. Yet it was enough to quiet accusations.

Democratic vice-presidential nominee Geraldine Ferraro similarly used television to answer accusations in 1984. She held a televised press conference to answer questions about her husband's business dealings and tax returns.

The first televised presidential debate was a feature of the 1960 election. By that time, most households had a television. Kennedy's careful grooming and practiced body language allowed viewers to focus on his presidential demeanor. His opponent, Richard Nixon, was still recovering from a severe case of the flu. While Nixon's substantive answers and debate skills made a favorable impression on radio listeners, television viewers' reaction to his sweaty appearance and obvious discomfort demonstrated that live television had the potential to make or break a candidate.

Television stations still enjoy wide viewership, but it has had to add the internet as a way for those viewers to find and watch them. Still, television remains an important source of news and entertainment whether viewers access that content via the airwaves or their internet connections.

However, just like newspapers and radio stations before it, local-television-station ownership has seen a significant consolidation in recent years. There are now 5 major American television networks who control 37% all local TV stations. The major networks are: Fox Broadcasting Company (Fox), National Broadcasting Company (NBC), CBS (formerly Columbia Broadcasting Company), American Broadcasting Company (ABC) and the CW Television Network.

A 2019 study found that these 5 conglomerates are reshaping local TV news. There are over 25-million viewers of nightly news programs. That's roughly 13% of the adult population of the U.S. This audience is far larger than national cable news programs such as Fox News and MSNBC.

This trend toward conglomerate (oligarch) ownership is triggering local stations to focus more on national politics rather than local politics. There is evidence that this trend is also making local stations slant more to the right politically. This is happening even though the stations are losing viewership.

The consolidation movement is also happening at the regional level. The Sinclair Broadcast Group (SBC) owns 191 TV stations that reach almost 40% of the U.S. population. SBC is now the nation's largest owner of local TV stations.

SBC has drawn attention for its conservative political leanings. For example, SBC stations aired 15 "exclusive" interviews with Donald Trump during the 2016 presidential campaign. After Trump was elected, SBC recruited a former Trump White House official as its chief political analyst. The company made all its local stations run this person's commentaries. And, all its anchors were ordered to read an identical script that repeated Trump's "fake news" claims.

Some researchers believe that one possible explanation for this type of shift to the right is that TV stations are just giving their audiences what they want. However, many other analysts think that the oligarchs that control these TV networks are influencing the content they provide to their viewers.

In addition to the shift to the conservative point-of-view, a concurrent development at local-TV stations is the increase in the amount of time they devote to national political news at the expense of local political news stories. Researchers have reported that this shift is as high as 25%. They also found that TV networks like SBC are allocating about 25% more broadcast time to national politics as their small competitors.

The reason for this swing to focusing on national political news may be as much financial as ideological. A local TV-news story that is produced by a local station requires a reporter, camera crew and editor. A national story produced by the parent company requires the same resources, but it can be distributed to all the local stations in the company's network. This offers a huge overall cost savings, and higher profits, for the owners of the network (oligarchs).

Whether the swing to the right is financially or politically motivated, it is clear these TV conglomerates have a lot of political power. One can easily imagine that the owners use that power to promote candidates and ideologies they prefer over those they don't. Also, a reduction in local political news makes it much more difficult for Americans to be properly informed about their local governments. Thus, making corruption and voter suppression much more likely.

There is no doubt in my mind that the Oligarchs behind the big TV networks are pushing their points-of-view as hard as they can through the content they run on their stations. Wouldn't you if you had that power? They can sway the outcomes of presidential campaigns in the direction they choose. There is considerable evidence that points to this conclusion. One wonders, are the regulators paying any attention? But then, the regulators are appointed by the politicians that are beholden to the Oligarchs. So, I guess it's no surprise.

The introduction of cable networks in the 1980s, and the rapid expansion of internet services in the late 1990s and early 2000s, provided many more options for Americans to access and consume the news. So many, in fact, that most of us are now suffering from a serious information overload. This has led to many viewers abandoning newscasts altogether, while just about everyone else has been separated into one of two news silos that are based on left-or-right-leaning politics (think NPR and Fox).

And, of course, there is social media as a prolific spreader of sometimes-accurate, not-accurate and fantastical news. In the 2008 presidential race, Barack Obama and his team expertly deployed an effective internet campaign strategy. His opponent, John McCain, did not. McCain relied on traditional media rather than social media. On election day, Obama had over 2-million Twitter followers while McCain had just 600,000. This made it clear that future elections would be fought primarily online. The 2020 elections cycle has borne this out.

There is no doubt that the news media has become biased and unreliable. Almost 70% of Americans responding to a 2020 Gallup poll indicated that they are more pessimistic than ever regarding the lack of objectivity in the news. They believe that this bias in news reporting is driven by the barely-concealed agendas of the oligarchs who own the news outlets. On the other hand, 84% of them believe that the institution of journalism is essential to a democracy.

Each successive poll over the past decade has shown that the American people are becoming increasingly polarized in the ways they think about the news media. In the recent Gallup poll referenced above, 49% of those surveyed said they think the media is very biased. About 75% believe the owners of media companies are influencing coverage. This is up 5% since 2017. And more alarmingly, 54% of them believe that reporters intentionally misrepresent facts, and 28% believe reporters make the facts up entirely.

Americans have lost confidence in the idea of an unbiased media. And, they believe news organizations actively incite the partisan divide. This shattered confidence in our news media is corrosive to our democracy.

Economic: The American economy was established by European settlers who came to the New World in pursuit of personal economic improvement. They crossed the Atlantic to America in the 16th, 17th, 18th and 19th centuries. These economic pioneers and their progeny transformed the early American agricultural economy into a sophisticated industrial economy.

In colonial times, farm families formed the backbone of the economy. They were engaged in handicraft production as well as farming. The colonial market economy was based on farming and on extracting and processing natural resources for local consumption. The major industrial activities included mining, gristmills and sawmills. The export of agricultural products was important to America's early economy.

The most important agricultural exports were raw and processed feed grains (wheat, Indian corn, rice, bread and flour), rice and tobacco. Tobacco was a major crop in the Chesapeake Bay region and rice a major crop in South Carolina. Dried-and-salted fish was also a significant export. North Carolina was the leading producer of naval stores, which included turpentine (used for lamps), rosin (candles and soap), tar (rope and wood preservative) and pitch (ships' hulls). Another export was potash that was derived from hardwood ashes and was used as a fertilizer and for making soap and glass.

The colonies depended on Britain for many finished goods. This was necessitated by the Navigation Acts of 1660. The Acts prohibited making many types of finished goods in the colonies. These laws achieved the intended purpose of creating a trade surplus for Britain. However, American shippers offset roughly half of the goods-trade deficit with revenues earned by shipping between ports within the British Empire.

Ship building accounted for 5% to 20% of total employment in the American colonies. About 45% of American-made ships were sold to foreigners. Exports and related services accounted for about 17% of income in the decade before the revolution. Just before the revolution, tobacco was about 25% of the value of American exports. Also, at the time of the revolution the colonies produced about 15% of the world's iron although the value of exported iron was small compared to grains and tobacco.

The mined American iron ores at that time were not in large deposits and were not all high quality. However, the huge forests of the New World provided adequate wood for making charcoal. Wood in Britain was becoming scarce and coke was beginning to be substituted for charcoal. However, coke made inferior iron. Britain encouraged colonial production of pig and bar iron, but it banned the construction of new colonial iron-fabrication shops in 1750. Colonist for the most part ignored the ban.

Settlement was sparse during the colonial period and transportation was severely limited by lack of improved roads. Towns were located on or near the coasts or navigable inland waterways. Even on improved roads, which were rare during the colonial period, wagon transport was very expensive. Twenty-five miles was the maximum economical distance for transporting low-value agricultural commodities to navigable waterways. In the few small cities, and among the larger plantations of South Carolina and Virginia, some necessities and virtually all luxuries were imported in return for tobacco, rice, and indigo exports.

By the 18th century, regional patterns of development had become clear. The New England colonies relied on shipbuilding and sailing to generate wealth. Plantations (most using slave labor) in Maryland, Virginia, and the Carolinas grew tobacco, rice, and indigo. The middle colonies of New York, Pennsylvania, New Jersey, and Delaware shipped general crops and furs. Except for the slaves, standards of living were even higher than in England itself.

Britain was in the early stages of the Industrial Revolution on the eve of American independence. British cottage industries and workshops provided finished goods for export to the colonies. At that time, half of the wrought iron, beaver hats, cordage, nails, linen, silk, and printed cotton produced in Britain were consumed by Britain's American colonies.

England is generally considered to be the birthplace of modern capitalism. However, Alan Greenspan (former Fed Chairman 1987 - 2006) in his new book "Capitalism in America: An Economic History of the Untied States" claims that, "The United States was the birthplace of the modern engines of capitalism, from mass production to franchising to mutual funds."

The 1800s saw the U.S. economy surge forward on a wave of industrialization and mechanized production. The iron, steel, lumber, precious metals, railroading, and petroleum industries boomed. By the late 1800s, known as the "Gilded Age", some enterprising American businessmen had become extremely wealthy. These "robber barons" included John D. Rockefeller, Andrew Carnegie, Cornelius Vanderbilt and Henry Ford. Most economic historians consider these robber barons to be America's first oligarchs. Their political contributions to politicians at all levels ensured that the laws of the land favored their plunder of the American economic system (sound familiar?). Their business practices were often considered ruthless and/or unethical.

Shortly after the start of the American Civil War (1861 - 1865), President Lincoln signed the Revenue Act (August 5, 1861). It was America's first personal-income tax. Desperately strapped for cash to pay for the Union war effort, Lincoln and Congress agreed to impose a 3% tax on annual incomes over $800 (about $21,000 in today's dollars).

The Constitution gave Congress the power to impose taxes and other levies on Americans. Most of these taxes were implemented in the form of excise taxes on specific goods or services like tobacco, tea and alcohol. The government also tried direct taxation by taxing things an individual owned. That didn't last, and the Federal Government went back to collecting excise taxes. The first income tax didn't last long either. It was repealed in 1872.

In 1894, Congress passed the Wilson-Gorman Tariff (aka the Income Tax Act of 1894). It reduced the tariffs on certain imports into the United States. The final version lowered duties slightly, but added a 2% federal income tax.

During the first decade of the 1900s, America's economy changed dramatically. It shifted from an agrarian to an industrial base. At that time, America was expanding its economic interests around the world. It became an emerging world power. This business expansion meant increased wealth as raw materials became cheaper to obtain. This drove prices down and consumption up.

Among the most prosperous businesses of the era were the oil, steel, textile, railroad and food-production industries. The decade was further marked by major technological innovations, such as the birth of the automobile and aviation industries. Americans who entered the century riding in horse-drawn buggies could, by the end of the decade, drive cars and fly in airplanes.

Many of the workers who were employed by the nation's expanding industries were immigrants. Nearly 9-million immigrants came to America during the decade, with most arrivals coming from Italy, Austria-Hungary, and Russia. The record year for immigration was 1907, when 1.3-million people took up American citizenship.

The early 1900s also saw American businesses expanding through mergers with companies in the same industry (horizontal integration), and by acquiring companies that supplied the raw materials, transportation and other functions needed for the expansion of the parent companies (vertical integration). This, to a large extent, eliminated competition. Americans became concerned about this consolidation of big business. Trusts, trade associations, cartels and pools were the tools used by big business to stifle their competitors. The public feared that these big-business groups would destroy America as the land of opportunity where it was possible for an individual to succeed through his or her own efforts.

Americans also witnessed the rise of the limited-liability corporation as the preferred organizational structure for large companies. Corporations that have since become fixtures in American life were founded then: Firestone Tire and Rubber Company (1900), United States Steel Company (1901), Quaker Oats Company (1901), J.C. Penney Company (1902), Pepsi-Cola Company (1902), Texaco (1903), Harley-Davidson (1907), Hershey (1908), and General Motors Corporation (1908).

The general prosperity of the decade made many Americans eager consumers, especially as companies began to spend more time and money on product advertising. The rise of big business and poor working conditions for common laborers led to increased tensions between employers and employees. Throughout the early 1900s, many workers joined organized labor unions. But, their efforts to improve pay and workplace conditions were often unsuccessful due to ruthless union busting by the big employers.

Several long and violent strikes occurred during the 1900s, and some of these work stoppages required government intervention to resolve the disputes. The great differences in the lifestyles of owners and workers was highly publicized, notably through the Anthracite Coal Strike of 1902. Nevertheless, union power became increasingly fragmented as worker unity was lost amid internal divisions based on race, gender, nationality, skill, and political beliefs. Of course, these fractures were expertly exploited by the big companies.

Although the early 1900s had a generally optimistic economic outlook, the confidence of many Americans was shaken by the sharp stock market drop in 1907. The first sign of financial panic was a run on the Knickerbocker Trust Company of New York, which collapsed the banking and credit system. Confidence was restored only because of the actions of the U.S. Treasury along with capitalists under the leadership of J.P. Morgan. They stabilized the banks and corporations with their own funds. The first decade of the century brought increasing commercialism to the lives of all Americans despite the gap between America's rich and poor.

1913 saw two important developments in the American economy: The Federal Reserve Bank was established and the federal income tax as we know it was signed into law. Both are still greatly effecting the lives of every American.

For the official history of the Federal Reserve (the Fed), let's turn to the Federal Reserve Website. In the interests of accuracy and relevance, the following history of the Fed is quoted directly from the site.

> *"To finance the American Revolution, the Continental Congress printed the new nation's first paper money. Known as "continentals," the fiat money notes were issued in such quantity they led to inflation, which, though mild at first, rapidly accelerated as the war progressed. Eventually, people lost faith in the notes, and the phrase 'Not worth a continental' came to mean 'utterly worthless'."*

"At the urging of then Treasury Secretary Alexander Hamilton, Congress established the First Bank of the United States, headquartered in Philadelphia, in 1791. It was the largest corporation in the country and was dominated by big banking and money interests. Many agrarian minded Americans uncomfortable with the idea of a large and powerful bank opposed it. When the bank's 20-year charter expired in 1811 Congress refused to renew it by one vote."

"By 1816, the political climate was once again inclined toward the idea of a central bank; by a narrow margin, Congress agreed to charter the Second Bank of the United States. But when Andrew Jackson, a central bank foe, was elected president in 1828, he vowed to kill it. His attack on its banker-controlled power touched a popular nerve with Americans, and when the Second Bank's charter expired in 1836, it was not renewed."

"State-chartered banks and unchartered 'free banks' took hold during this period, issuing their own notes, redeemable in gold or specie. Banks also began offering demand deposits to enhance commerce. In response to a rising volume of check transactions, the New York Clearinghouse Association was established in 1853 to provide a way for the city's banks to exchange checks and settle accounts."

"During the Civil War, the National Banking Act of 1863 was passed, providing for nationally chartered banks, whose circulating notes had to be backed by U.S. government securities. An amendment to the act required taxation on state bank notes but not national bank notes, effectively creating a uniform currency for the nation."

"Despite taxation on their notes, state banks continued to flourish due to the growing popularity of demand deposits, which had taken hold during the Free Banking Era. Although the National Banking Act of 1863 established some measure of currency stability for the growing nation, bank runs and financial panics continued to plague the economy. In 1893, a banking panic triggered the worst depression the United States had ever seen, and the economy stabilized only after the intervention of financial mogul J.P. Morgan. It was clear that the nation's banking and financial system needed serious attention."

"In 1907, a bout of speculation on Wall Street ended in failure, triggering a particularly severe banking panic. J.P. Morgan was again called upon to avert disaster. By this time, most Americans were *calling for reform of the banking system, but the structure of that reform was cause for deep division among the country's citizens. Conservatives and powerful 'money trusts' in the big eastern cities were vehemently opposed by 'progressives'. But there was a growing consensus among all Americans that a central banking authority was needed to ensure a healthy banking system and provide for an elastic currency."*

"The Aldrich-Vreeland Act of 1908, passed as an immediate response to the panic of 1907, provided for emergency currency issue during crises. It also established the national Monetary Commission to search for a long-term solution to the nation's banking and financial problems. Under the leadership of Senator Nelson Aldrich, the commission developed a banker-controlled plan. William Jennings Bryan and other progressives fiercely attacked the plan; they wanted a central bank under public, not banker, control. The 1912 election of Democrat Woodrow Wilson killed the Republican Aldrich plan, but the stage was set for the emergence of a decentralized central bank."

"Though not personally knowledgeable about banking and financial issues, Woodrow Wilson solicited expert advice from Virginia Representative Carter Glass, soon to become the chairman of the House Committee on Banking and Finance, and from the Committee's expert advisor, H. Parker Willis, formerly a professor of economics at Washington and Lee University. Throughout most of 1912, Glass and Willis labored over a central bank proposal, and by December 1912, they presented Wilson with what would become, with some modifications, the Federal Reserve Act."

"From December 1912 to December 1913, the Glass-Willis proposal was hotly debated, molded and reshaped. By December 23, 1913, when President Woodrow Wilson signed the Federal Reserve Act into law, it stood as a classic example of compromise—a decentralized central bank that balanced the competing interests of private banks and populist sentiment."

"Before the new central bank could begin operations, the Reserve Bank Operating Committee, comprised of Treasury Secretary William McAdoo, Secretary of Agriculture David Houston, and Comptroller of the Currency John Skelton Williams, had the arduous task of building a working institution around the bare bones of the new law. But, by November 16, 1914, the 12 cities chosen as sites for regional Reserve

Banks were open for business, just as hostilities in Europe erupted into World War I."

World War I (1914 – 1918) drove a 44-months-long economic boom in the United States. It started with the purchase of U.S. war materiel by European countries already engaged in the struggle and progressed to the acquisition of these same types of goods by the U.S. Government when it entered the war. The government-directed mobilization of America's economy was exceptional. Many Americans became convinced that the Federal Government could play a positive role in the national economy.

This belief was crucial to solving the problems the country faced when it was confronted with the Great Depression (1929 – 1933). The economic precedents set during WW I influenced how Americans addressed this existential threat. The concept of creating new government agencies and programs to help America exit the crisis were rooted in the war.

For example, the Federal Government hired young men to work on conservation projects around the country (the Civilian Conservation Corps—CCC). Recruits enjoyed the benefits of military-style training in a civilian venue. The new Agricultural Adjustment Administration reflected the structure and policies of the WW I Food Administration. And, the National Industrial Recovery Act reflected ideas that were developed at the WW I War Industries Board.

Lasting from October 1929 to March 1933, the Great Depression was the worst economic downturn in the history of the industrialized world. A U.S. stock market crash started the chaos when it sent Wall Street into a panic that wiped out the capital of millions of investors and led to the failure of over 4,000 banks. To counteract Wall Street excesses, Congress passed the Glass-Stegall Act in 1933. It essentially separated commercial banking from investment banking, and it created the Federal Deposit Insurance Corporation (FDIC). The Act was hotly debated before President Roosevelt signed it into law.

Most liberal historians agree that Franklin D. Roosevelt's New Deal of 1933 to 1939 was what brought America out of the Great Depression. The New Deal was a matrix of federal policies and programs, financial reforms, regulations and public-work projects that were put in place by the Roosevelt Administration and Congress. On the other hand, conservative economic historians believe that it was America's entry into World War II that provided the economic stimulus that was needed for the recovery.

It was probably both the New Deal and WW II that did the trick. In any event, it was "big government" that got the job done. Using economic tools like government-funded employment and government-funded projects that contributed to the common good is now a proven method of recovering from economic slumps and crashes.

On the eve of America's entry into World War II (December 7, 1941), America was still recovering from the Great Depression. The unemployment rate had been as high as 25%. American businesses were still reeling from the effects of the depressed economy. Bankruptcies were common and the average American's standard of living was 60% lower than before the stock market crash of 1929.

America's entry into WW II was the most remarkable mobilization of an all-but-dormant economy in the history of the world. During the war, 17-million new civilian jobs were created in addition to the 16-million "jobs" in the military, industrial productivity increased by 96% and corporate profits after taxes doubled. American factories were retooled to produce goods to support the war effort and almost overnight the unemployment rate dropped to around 10%. Women were hired in great numbers to take over the positions on the assembly lines vacated by the men who went off to fight the war.

The Federal Government emerged from WW II as a superstar economic player. It proved that it could regulate U.S. economic activity and significantly control the economy through spending and consumption. American industry was revitalized by WW II, and many sectors remained focused on defense production (aerospace, electronics, atomics, etc.) after the war.

Strengthened by the war beyond even its pre-depression-era level, organized labor became a major counterbalance to both the government and private industry. After the war, rapid scientific and technological changes continued. That intensified trends that had begun during the Great Depression and created a permanent expectation of continued innovation on the part of many citizens, scientists, engineers and government officials.

The substantial increases in personal income and quality of life during the war led many Americans to anticipate permanent improvements in their lifestyles. Outside America, the war's global scale severely damaged every major economy in the world. However, America enjoyed unprecedented economic and political power after the war ended in 1945.

The Serviceman's Readjustment Act of 1944 authorized the GI Bill. Returning American veterans took advantage of the GI Bill in droves. By the time the benefits of the original bill ran out, 8-million veterans had taken advantage of it to go to college, get technical-job training and to buy a home. This was critical to the development of the middle class. The GI Bill was so successful following WWII that is was reinstated following the Korean and Vietnam Wars. It was further expanded after September 11, 2001.

In the years following World War II, America experienced extraordinary economic growth. It returned to prosperity and it became the richest country in the world. More-and-more Americans considered themselves to be "middle class" as the GDP grew to over $540-billion in 1960 ($4.7-trillion in 2020 dollars) from $103-billion in 1940 ($1.9-trillion in 2020 dollars). The number of automobiles quadrupled from the end of the war through 1955. Affordable mortgages for veterans stimulated a housing boom. And, the increase in defense spending as the Cold War heated up added significantly to the growth.

During and after the WWII, big companies got considerably bigger. A new wave of mergers and acquisitions rolled across the country in the 1950s. Companies with holdings in several industries (known as conglomerates) showed the way. For example, International Telephone and Telegraph (IT&T), acquired Sheraton Hotels, Continental Baking, Hartford Fire Insurance and Avis Rent-a-Car. The nascent franchise craze gave the country McDonald's fast-food restaurants. Large corporations also developed holdings overseas where labor costs were often lower.

As American companies changed, the lives of workers likewise transformed. For the first time, more Americans worked in jobs that provided services than produced goods. By 1956, more Americans held white-collar jobs rather than blue-collar. They worked as corporate managers, teachers, salespersons and office workers. Some companies guaranteed an annual wage, long-term employment contracts, company-paid health insurance, defined-benefit retirement plans and other popular benefits. Labor militancy was undermined by these changes and some class distinctions began to fade.

On the other hand, the lives of American farmers were not so rosy. Productivity gains led to agricultural consolidation. Farming became a big business and family farms found it difficult to compete. An increasing number of farmers left the land for jobs in the cities.

The Federal Aid Highway Act of 1956 (popularly known as the National Interstate and Defense Highways Act) created new highways across America.

The Act called for $25-billion ($239-billion in 2020 dollars) to build more than 41,000 miles of limited-access roadways to link major cities together and to their suburbs. It was the largest public works expenditure in U.S. history. During the 1960s and 1970s, turmoil in America and around the world grew to an alarming level. The increasingly confrontational Cold War and the hot war in Vietnam significantly contributed to this angst. Added to this were social conflicts in many countries. New nations were created while insurgent movements sought to overthrow existing governments. America was challenged by new economic powerhouses. And, international economic relationships became very important in a world that increasingly recognized that growth and expansion could come from economic development as well as military power.

The post-war prosperity was broadly shared. Incomes grew rapidly and at roughly the same rate for everyone on the economic ladder. Between the late 1940s and late 1970s, incomes doubled (adjusted for inflation). The gap between those at the top of the income ladder and those on the middle and lower rungs—while substantial—did not change much during this period.

In the early 1960s, President John F. Kennedy (1961 – 1963) led a more-activist administration than most of his predecessors. As president, he sought to accelerate economic growth by increasing government spending and cutting taxes. He pressed for medical support for the elderly, aid for inner cities and increased funds for education.

Many of Kennedy's proposals were not enacted, although his vision of sending Americans abroad to help developing nations did materialize with the creation of the Peace Corps. Kennedy also stepped up American space exploration culminating in America's 1969 moon landing.

President Kennedy's 1963 assassination prompted Congress to enact much of his legislative agenda. His successor, Lyndon Johnson (1963-1969) sought to build a "Great Society" by spreading the benefits of America's thriving economy to more citizens. Federal spending increased dramatically as the government launched such new programs as Medicare (health care for the elderly), Food Stamps (food assistance for the poor) and numerous education initiatives.

The military's budget also increased as American's presence in Vietnam grew and the Cold War continued unabated. What had started as a small military action in Vietnam under Kennedy mushroomed into a significant military initiative during Johnson's presidency. Ironically, spending on 3 wars—the war on poverty, the war in Vietnam and the Cold War—contributed to prosperity in the short term, but by the end of the 1960s the government's failure to raise taxes to pay for these efforts led to accelerating inflation that eroded this prosperity.

The Organization of Petroleum Exporting Countries (OPEC) pushed energy prices rapidly higher and created shortages with its 1973 – 1974 oil embargo. Energy prices stayed high after the embargo ended. This contributed to inflation and caused an increase in the unemployment rate. Federal budget deficits grew and foreign competition intensified. This caused the stock market to fall.

The Vietnam War dragged on until 1975. President Richard Nixon (1969-1974) resigned under a cloud of impeachment charges in 1974. And, Americans were taken hostage at the U.S. embassy in Tehran and held for more than a year. America seemed unable to control events—including economic affairs. Our trade deficit swelled as low-priced and frequently high-quality imports of everything from automobiles to steel to semiconductors flooded into the United States.

The American people expressed their discontent with the federal government's policies of the 1970s through the election of President Ronald Reagan in 1980. Reagan championed an economic program that was based on the theory of supply-side economics. This theory mandated a reduction in the marginal tax rates to encourage people to work harder. This in turn, in theory, would lead to more saving and investment. And, this would result in more production and a stimulation of the economy. Reagan's "supply-side" and "trickle-down" economic theories have been proven to be invalid.

After his election, President Reagan championed the deregulation of most industries. This, coupled with the emphasis on shareholder capitalism, began a long degradation of the lot of millions of American workers. Almost every American worker's livelihood and job security was negatively affected by these trends. I was personally effected by this change. As a pilot for United Airlines at the time, I witnessed firsthand how a revered and much-sought-after profession could be significantly damaged by shareholder capitalism.

The central theme of Reagan's national agenda was his belief that the federal government had become too big and invasive. In the early 1980s, the Reagan administration pushed through a series of tax cuts and significant slashes in social programs. Reagan also launched a campaign to reduce or eliminate government environmental, consumer and workplace regulations.

Largely due to Reagan's policies, America endured a deep recession in 1982. Business bankruptcies rose 50% over 1981. Farmers were especially hard hit as agricultural exports declined and crop prices fell. Interest rates also rose dramatically and hyperinflation reared its ugly head. But the recession, combined with falling oil prices and the Federal Reserve's tight control of money and credit, helped to curb runaway inflation.

The economy rebounded in 1983 and the United States entered one of the longest periods of sustained economic growth since World War II. The annual inflation rate remained under 5% through 1987. Although the Fed would like to keep the inflation rate under 3%, 5% was considered just fine for the times.

However, serious problems remained. Farmers' suffering was compounded by serious droughts in 1986 and 1988. Federal deficits soared throughout the 1980s. The federal budget deficit rose from $74-billion ($232-billion in 2020 dollars) in 1980 to $221-billion ($523-billion in 2020 dollars) in 1986. However, it was reduced to $150-billion ($342-billion in 2020 dollars) in 1987. The U.S. trade deficit hit a record $152-billion ($382-billion in 2020 dollars) that same year. A stock market crash in the autumn of 1987 led many to question the stability of the economy.

The 1980s also saw some significant changes in the economic rules-of-the-game. These "heads-I-win, tails-you-loose" rules are still with us and they have created severely-negative effects on the American economy and culture. One of the most-onerous new rules was the mandate for CEOs to focus on shareholder capitalism rather than stakeholder capitalism. This led to a total focus on the bottom line and short-term growth in an attempt to maximize returns to shareholders at the expense of the common good, employees, customers, suppliers and retirees.

In his illuminating book "How Money Became Dangerous: The Inside Story of Our Turbulent Relationship With Money" (Harper Collins 2019), Christopher Varelas (former head of Citi Bank's National Investment Bank) tells us that in the 1980s, "…our financial system became increasingly complicated, with each evolution moving the world of money further beyond the understanding of the general public." The 1980s also saw the big banks switch from private to public ownership. Venerable firms such as L. F. Rothschild and Bear, Stearns & Company (and others) decided to switch from private to public hands by going public on the New York Stock Exchange.

Once public, these banks were no longer run by partners with skin in game. Instead, CEOs and other employees began to maximize their compensation through performance-based incentives. When they made large and risky bets on the stock market and other investments, they were no longer betting their own money but that of their shareholders. This radically changed the risk/reward strategies used by these firms. It was now "heads I win, tails the firm and shareholders loose".

The first Gulf War started in mid-1990 and the U.S. economy soon slid into recession. The war ended in early 1991and the economy recovered. Because of the war and the slowing economy, the federal budget deficit began heading upward again. Although the stock market recovered, the financial industry was particularly plagued with problems. Numerous savings institutions, banks and insurance companies either failed or they were in such an unstable state that they were taken over by the federal government. Well into the 1990's, credit-market and other problems lingered on. By contrast, other sectors of the economy (i.e., computers, aerospace and export industries) generally showed signs of continuing growth.

After the relatively mild 1990 – 1991 recession, the unemployment rate peaked at 7.8% in mid-1992. Job growth was offset by layoffs in the defense industry. However, payrolls grew in 1992 and experienced robust growth through 2000.

In 1999, the Glass-Steagall Act was replaced by the Gramm-Leach-Bliley Act. This happened in the wake of several changes in the structure and operations of the big banks. The Gramm-Leach-Bliley Act (aka Financial Services Modernization Act) essentially deregulated the financial-services industry by removing barriers that separated commercial banking from investment banking, merchant banking and insurance underwriting. The big banks got bigger as they massively increased their speculative holdings (like collateralized securities) and acquired smaller banks. This led to the crisis caused by the bursting of the housing bubble in 2005.

There were 2 recessions in the 2000s. The first one ran from 2001 to 2003 and is commonly referred to as the "Post-9/11 Recession". It ended the late 1990s stock-market boom. In 2001, 1.7-million jobs were lost. In 2002, an additional 508,000 jobs were lost. However, 105,000 jobs were gained back in 2003. Unemployment rose from 4.2% in February 2001 to 5.5% in November 2001, but did not peak until June 2003 at 6.3%, after which it declined to 5% by mid-2005.

The second recession began in December 2007 and it continued until 2009. It is commonly referred to as the "Great Recession". It was was caused by a combination of factors that developed in the financial system, along with a series of triggering events that began with the bursting of the United States housing bubble in 2005.

During this recession, millions of Americans lost their jobs causing many of them to miss home-mortgage payments. The resulting foreclosures caused home prices to fall precipitously as the new jobless walked away from their mortgages. Most of these mortgages were bundled into "mortgage-backed securities" and sold to unwary investors. Major American investments banks failed and the Federal Government bailed out many others in 2008 as a response to the "subprime-mortgage crisis". Most economic experts think the Great Recession was caused by a combination of homeowners paying down debt instead of spending on consumer goods and banks that were unable to provide funding for businesses.

In 2010, the job market began its recovery from the most-severe downturn since the Great Depression. And, the average wage (adjusted for inflation) rose modestly. However, the recovery was achingly slow. By 2015, the economy was growing at a respectable 2.9%—its strongest growth since 2005. In 2016, the GDP growth rate was 4.5%.

The U.S. GDP grew by 4.1% in 2019 to $21.4-trillion. The economy grew by an average annual rate of 2.2% between 2009 and 2019. In 2019, the unemployment rate was at a very-low 3.6% compared to the average unemployment rate of 5.8% from 1948 to 2019.

However, the Covid-19 pandemic significantly disrupted the U.S. economy beginning in early 2020. By April 2020, the official unemployment rate was 14.7%, but it is believed that the true rate is much higher and it is expected to increase as we move into 2021. And, as we all know, the American economy has been working for only about 5% of Americans for the last 4 decades.

According to the U.S. Bureau of Economic Analysis, in the second quarter of 2020 America's real Gross Domestic Product (GDP) fell at an annualized rate of 32.9%. *Fortune Magazine* estimates that almost 100,000 businesses have permanently shut down due to the pandemic. And the Pew Research Center tells us, "Household incomes have grown only modestly in this century, and household wealth has not returned to its pre-Great-Recession level. Economic inequality, whether measured through the gaps in income or wealth between richer and poorer households, continues to widen."

From the end of World War II (1945) into the 1970s, America enjoyed substantial economic growth and broadly-shared prosperity. Incomes grew rapidly at roughly the same rate no matter where one was on the income ladder. They doubled (in inflation-adjusted terms) between the late 1940s and early 1970s. The gaps between those at the top of the income ladder and those on the middle and lower rungs was substantial, but they didn't change much during those years.

U.S. economic growth slowed and the income gap widened beginning in the 1970s. Middle-and-lower-class income growth slowed sharply while incomes at the top continued to grow robustly. The concentration of income at the very top of the distribution rose to levels last seen nearly a century ago, during the "Roaring Twenties" (1920s).

Wealth (the value of a household's property and financial assets, minus its debts) is now much more highly concentrated than income. The best survey data show that the share of wealth held by the top 1% of Americans rose from 30% in 1989 to 39% in 2016. The share held by the bottom 90% fell from 33% to 23%.

Today, the wealth and income gaps in our country are deterring most Americans' (95%) shot at the American dream. The Founders baked into the Declaration of Independence and the Constitution the promise of the pursuit (practice) of happiness for every American, not just a privileged few.

Culture: America's culture has had many influences over the years. The culture around the time of America's Declaration of Independence was primarily the result of the mixing of English, other northern-European, Native American and African cultures. By the 20th century, the list of cultures that are still part of American culture also included Latin American, Asian and Pacific Island.

"Culture encompasses religion, food, what we wear, how we wear it, our language, marriage, music, what we believe is right or wrong, how we sit at the table, how we greet visitors, how we behave with loved ones, and a million other things," said Cristina De Rossi, an anthropologist at Barnet and Southgate College in London. American culture is certainly all this and a lot more.

America has been characterized as a melting pot. It has one of the most culturally-diverse cultures on the planet. Just as cultures from around the world have influenced American culture, American culture has influenced the world.

America also has a unique political culture. A political culture is based on the shared beliefs and attitudes of its members that define public and private governance. Political culture builds community and facilitates communication. It allows people to share an understanding of how and why political events, actions and experiences occur.

A political culture's widely-shared values, norms and beliefs define the relationship between the government and the governed, and how citizens relate to one another. Beliefs about economic life are part of the political culture because politics effect economics and economics effect politics.

Part of the American culture is what we generally refer to as the "American Dream". It is the belief that every American has the freedom and opportunity to secure a better life for themselves and their children. The manifold rags-to-riches stories that have been written throughout America's history have contributed to the American political culture. Consider Abraham Lincoln's story of the achievement of great success even though he was born in a log cabin.

There were at least 3 political cultures in colonial America. They were based on the cultures of the British Isles and the Netherlands. They evolved into unique cultures that still exist today. For example, a moralistic political culture existed in New England. It was characterized by an emphasis on community and civic virtue over individualism.

The American political culture has evolved since colonial times. Many aspects of it have changed, but in many ways, it has remained remarkably the same. One thing that has been constant is the special emphasis American political culture puts on hard work. The following are other features of America's political culture that have remained fairly constant over the years:

- *DEMOCRACY:* Americans believe their flavor of democracy should be conducted by the people and for the people. They think their elected officials should be accountable to the people, and that citizens have the responsibility to choose their officials thoughtfully and wisely.

- *LIBERTY:* To most people, "liberty" means that they have the right to do what they want as long as they aren't abusing another's rights.

- *EQUALITY:* This generally translates as "equality of opportunity," not absolute equality. However, the belief is growing in the need for better equality of resources with which to pursue equal opportunities.

- *THE RULE OF LAW:* American political culture also includes the belief that government is based on a body of law applied equally and fairly to all citizens. Although most Americans today still believe that this is the way it should be, the reality is quite different.

- *CAPITALISM:* The American Dream includes beliefs in the right to own private property and to compete freely in open markets that have as little government involvement as possible.

- *INDIVIDUALISM:* The individual's rights are valued above those of the state (government); individual initiative and responsibility are strongly encouraged. This thinking is also currently evolving towards more emphasis on the common good.

- *NATIONALISM:* Most Americans are proud of their past. This value includes the belief that we are stronger and more virtuous than other nations.

Today's American political culture has been described as "divisive", "toxic", "dysfunctional" and "crazy". It is polarized in many ways: urban-rural, left-right, conservative-liberal, rich-middle class and rich-poor to name a few. The polarization is created by 2 main flavors of highly-evolved propaganda. The good news is that America's political culture continues to evolve. I believe there is hope that we can bend the arc of our political culture to a more-positive-and-productive trajectory.

Climate: Experiments that investigated the possibility that human-produced carbon dioxide (CO_2) and other gases could collect in the atmosphere and trap heat began in the 1800s. These experiments were met with more curiosity than alarm. Early interest in what we now call "climate change" focused on the ice ages the Earth has experienced and the possibility that the planet was building up "greenhouse gases" that could cause our climate to warm.

By the late 1950s, CO2 readings offered some of the first data to corroborate the global-warming theory. In the 1960s, other theories of climate change were advanced. They ranged from solar variation to volcanism. By the late 1960s, the evidence for the greenhouse effect of CO2 became increasingly convincing. Some scientists also pointed out that human activities that suspended solid particles and water droplets in the atmospheric could also have cooling effects.

During the 1970s, scientists studying the phenomena increasingly favored the global-warming theory. Due to the improving fidelity of computer models and observational work that confirmed the ice ages, a consensus position was formed in the 1990s. It was generally agreed by the scientific community that greenhouse gases were involved in most climate changes and human-caused emissions were bringing noticeable global warming.

Since the 1990s, expanding scientific research on climate change has included multiple disciplines. This research has greatly increased our understanding of the causes of climate change. Most scientists believe that climate change causes significant and lasting effects. We now know that climate change is caused by many influences that include oceanic processes, volcanic eruptions, biotic processes, variations in solar radiation, plate tectonics and human alterations of the natural world.

The climate-change movement has its roots in the environmental movement. Concern for the impact of humans on the environment dates to ancient times. Soil conservation was practiced in China, India, and Peru as early as 2,000 years ago. Pollution was associated with the spread of diseases in Europe between the late 14th century and the mid-16th century. However, such concerns did not give rise to widespread environmental activism until the first Earth Day in 1970.

A collection of non-governmental organizations power the climate-change movement. They are engaged in activism on a global scale. It is a subset of the broader environmental movement. But, given its scope, strength, and activities many regard it as a new social movement itself. The climate-change movement has rapidly evolved in the first decades of the 21st century.

Climate-change activism began in the 1990s. That's when the major environmental organizations became involved in the discussions about climate change. In the 2000s, several climate-change-specific organizations were founded, such as 350.org, Energy Action Coalition, and the Global Call for Climate Action.

The 2009 United Nations Climate Change Conference in Copenhagen was the first United Nations Framework Convention on Climate Change (UNFCCC) summit in which the climate-change movement started showing its mobilization power on a large scale. Over 100,000 people attended a march in Copenhagen on December 12, 2009. They called for a global agreement on climate. Activism spread rapidly beyond Copenhagen. Over subsequent years, more than 5,400 rallies and demonstrations took place around the world.

The climate-change movement convened its largest single event in 2014 when it mobilized 400,000 activists in New York during the People's Climate March (plus several thousand more in other cities). Organized by the People's Climate Movement, marchers demanded climate action from the global leaders gathered for the 2014 UN Climate Summit.

Since 2014, growing segments of the climate-change movement (especially in the United States) have been advocating for an international economic response to climate change. Their goal is to significantly reduce carbon emissions and transition to 100% clean energy faster than the free market is likely to allow.

In 2015 and 2016, The Climate Mobilization movement (a grassroots environmental-advocacy group) led popular climate-change-awareness campaigns in the U.S. In July 2016, activists succeeded in getting a World War II-scale climate-change-mobilization program adopted by the Democratic Party's national platform. Since 2018, inspired by Greta Thunberg, children and students in at least 270 cities have taken part in school strikes for the climate.

Groups advocating for a sustainable environment are now an important part of the climate-change movement. They want to see the widespread use of clean energy, conservation and the removal of carbon from the atmosphere. The faith community is split on its beliefs about climate change. The more-conservative faiths seem to be mostly climate-change deniers while the more-liberal churches support organizations like the Global Catholic Climate Movement.

The Paris Agreement Under the United Nations Framework Convention on Climate Change (aka Paris Climate Agreement, Paris Agreement, Paris Accord or COP21) was adopted in December 2015. It aims to reduce the emission of greenhouse gases that contribute to climate change. The agreement focuses on accelerating and intensifying the actions and investments needed for a sustainable low-carbon future.

For the first time, the Paris Agreement brought all nations into a common cause to undertake ambitious efforts to combat climate change and adapt to its effects. The agreement also called for assistance for developing countries to comply with it. The Paris Agreement charted a new course in the global climate-change effort.

Shortly after taking office in 2017, President Trump withdrew the U.S. from the Paris Agreement. Trump stated that "The Paris Accord will undermine the U.S. economy," and "it puts the U.S. at a permanent disadvantage." If the withdrawal takes effect, the U.S. will be the only UNFCCC member state that is not a signatory to the Paris Agreement.

The withdrawal was celebrated by most members of the Republican Party. However, international reactions to the departure from across the political spectrum were overwhelmingly negative. The decision received significant criticism from religious groups, businesses, political leaders of all parties, environmentalist, scientists and Americans from all walks of life.

Following Trump's announcement, the governors of several U.S. states formed the United States Climate Alliance to continue to advance the objectives of the Paris Agreement at the state level despite Trump's withdrawal. As of July 1, 2019, 24 states and Puerto Rico had joined the alliance. Similar commitments have also been expressed by other state governors, mayors, and businesses. President-Elect Biden has promised to put America back into the accord on his first day in office.

The September 2019 Global Week for the Future included a series of international strikes and protests to demand that action be taken to address climate change. A second wave of protests took place later in September in which an estimated 2-million people took part in over 2,400 protests around the world.

In 2020, President Trump's and the Republican Party's assault on the efforts to curtail global warming are continuing unabated. In addition to withdrawing from the Paris Accords, the Trump Administration has also abolished and/or gutted many other environmental laws, policies and regulations. All in the face of the obvious fact that global warming is changing our climate. Climate change is already having dire consequences: more-frequent flooding in the central US, a record number of hurricanes and tropical storms hitting the U.S., a longer and more-costly wildfire season in the West and droughts across the Great Plains.

In addition to these ill-advised moves, President Trump has directed the U.S. intelligence services to target climate-change activists as domestic terrorists. This includes investigating environmental activists and climate-change organizations and placing them on national watch lists. This makes it more difficult for them to board airplanes (thus curtailing their activism) and it could instigate local law enforcement monitoring. Unknown actors also secretly hired professional hackers to launch phishing and hacking attacks against the climate activists who were organizing the #ExxonKnew campaign. These tactics are being deployed to intimidate climate-change activists and could lead to the criminalization of the movement by a Republican administration.

The political right has criticized climate-change activists and pro-climate politicians for proclaiming that we have only 12-years to stop climate change. Scientists say the situation is in some ways worse than that. We can solve our climate crisis if we urgently move to zero emissions and 100%-clean energy. But, we need national leadership and a real commitment to saving the planet for our children and grandchildren.

Infrastructure: At the time of the American revolution, the country's infrastructure was made up primarily of canals and roads. The canals provided affordable regional travel and shipping. The roads mainly served local communities. Ports and lighthouses were integral to sea transportation. A few big towns and cities had aqueducts as components of local water-distribution systems. However, sewer systems were still rare.

Although the first official notice of a postal service in the colonies appeared in 1633, America's communications infrastructure was formalized in 1775 (during the Second Continental Congress) when Benjamin Franklin was appointed as our first Postmaster General. The Post Office Department was created in 1792 with the passage of the Postal Service Act. It was elevated to a cabinet-level department in 1872.

The United States Constitution contains the Postal Clause or the Postal Power (Article I, Section 8, Clause 7). It empowered Congress "To establish Post Offices and Post Roads." The Post Office has the constitutional authority to designate mail routes; construct or designate post offices; and carry, deliver and regulate the mail. The Postal Reorganization Act of 1970 authorized a name change to the United States Postal Service and made it an independent agency of the Executive Branch.

From colonial times to the mid-1880s, America's roads were mainly dirt-and-mud paths. Then, for a short time, roads were paved with wooden blocks. Early turnpike companies built these roads and there was often a toll charge of one-to-two cents per horse. By the late 1800s, America was paving its roads with tar. One of the first tar-paved roads was Pennsylvania Avenue in Washington D.C.

Waterways and canals linked the frontier with the eastern cities. Produce moved on small boats along canals and rivers from the farms to the ports. Large steamships carried goods and people from port to port. In 1817, the New York State Legislature approved construction of the Erie Canal. The bill authorized $7-million ($140-million in 2020 dollars) for construction of the 363-mile long waterway. It linked the Hudson River in Albany to Lake Erie in Buffalo.

Railroads appeared on the American scene in 1815 when the first railroad charter was granted to Col. John Stevens. However, the Baltimore & Ohio Railroad beat him to market by opening a 14-mile-long line between Baltimore and Ellicott, MD in 1830. The Baltimore & Ohio grew to become one of America's largest railroads.

In addition to the railroads, the 1850s also saw the introduction of the electrical telegraph in America. In 1861, the Western Union Telegraph Company linked the nation's eastern and western telegraph networks at Salt Lake City, Utah. That linkup completed a transcontinental telegraph line that for the first time allowed virtually instantaneous communication between Washington, D.C., and San Francisco.

In 1876, Alexander Graham Bell made the first successful telephone transmission of clear speech. Soon, a bell and switch-hook were added. Early telephones took advantage of the central-exchange principle. American Telephone and Telegraph (AT&T) was founded in 1885. It built and managed a local telephone network in New York City. AT&T added a long-distance network between New York and Chicago in 1892.

The Edison Illuminating Company was established by Thomas Edison in 1880. It constructed electrical-generating stations in lower Manhattan. They served 1 square mile with 6 "jumbo dynamos" housed at Pearl Street Station. The company was the prototype for other local electric companies that were established in the United States during the 1880s.

The first sewer systems in America were built in the late 1850s in Chicago and Brooklyn. The first sewage-treatment plant using chemical precipitation was built in Worcester, MA in 1890. The technique for the purification of drinking water by use of compressed liquefied chlorine gas was developed in 1910 by U.S. Army Major Carl Rogers Darnall. His work became the basis for present-day municipal water-purification systems

In 1936, the Hoover Dam was completed 5 years after construction was begun. Building it used over 20,000-tons of steel and 5-million barrels of concrete. It harnessed the power of the Colorado River for irrigation and the generation of electrical power. The dam proved that infrastructure projects could have immediate benefits for the U.S. economy. The project employed 21,000 people at the height of the Great Depression. America invested some $49-million ($767-million is 2020 dollars) in this addition to the country's infrastructure.

By the early 1900s, the country's total rail mileage had increased to over 193,346 miles from 163,597 in 1890. By this time, railroads had reached economic supremacy. They connected cities with the tiniest of hamlets and trains dominated American commerce in every possible way.

The railroad streamliner craze that was so prevalent during the 1930s had slowed down by the late 1940s. Route mileage peaked at 254,251 miles (roughly the distance from the Earth to the Moon) in 1916, but it had fallen to 139,679 miles by 2011. Railroad employment peaked at 2.1-million in 1920. Due to modernization and a huge reduction in traffic, railroad employment fell to 1.2-million by 1950 and 215,000 by 2010.

Although the Wright Brothers flew the first manned, powered and controllable airplane in 1903, there was only one airline founded before World War I—the St. Petersburg-Tampa Airboat Line in 1914. It took the technological impetus of WWI and another decade of development before today's major airlines were founded—Delta Airlines in 1925, United Airlines in 1926 and American Airlines in 1930.

The Kelly Airmail Act of 1925 greatly increased competition in the nascent airline industry. It soon led to the carrying of mail, people and airfreight. The Act facilitated the establishment of a profitable commercial-airline industry. By the end of the 1920s, there were almost 200 commercial airports in the U.S.

In 1934, the Department of Commerce renamed its Aeronautics Branch the Bureau of Air Commerce. This reflected the growing importance of aviation to the nation. In one of its first acts, the Bureau encouraged a group of airlines to establish the first air traffic control centers (Newark, Cleveland and Chicago) to provide enroute air traffic control. In 1936, the Bureau of Air Commerce took over air-traffic control.

President Franklin Roosevelt signed the Civil Aeronautics Act in 1938 to ensure a federal focus on aviation safety. The legislation established the independent Civil Aeronautics Authority (CAA) with a 3-member Air Safety Board. It conducted accident investigations and recommended ways of preventing aviation accidents. The legislation also expanded the government's role in civil aviation by giving the CAA the power to regulate airline fares and determine the routes individual carriers served.

In 1940, President Roosevelt split the CAA into two agencies—the Civil Aeronautics Administration (which went back to the Department of Commerce) and the Civil Aeronautics Board (CAB). The CAA retained responsibility for airman and aircraft certification, safety enforcement and airway development. The CAB was responsible for safety rulemaking, accident investigation and the economic regulation of the airlines.

On the eve of America's entry into World War II, for defense purposes the CAA extended its air-traffic control system to include operation of airport towers. In the postwar era, air-traffic control became a permanent federal responsibility at most commercial airports. The postwar era also witnessed the advent of jet transports.

In the mid-1900s, petroleum-powered vehicles became the main form of transport in the U.S. Gas-driven trucks, cars, motor coaches and airplanes began to supersede rail transport. Public transport declined with increasing use of private vehicles. The standards of roads improved. Virtually all public roads in America were sealed by the 1970s.

The Pennsylvania Turnpike was the first long-distance rural freeway in the United States. It opened in 1940. The Interstate Highway System was authorized by the Federal-Aid Highway Act of 1956. Most of the system was completed between 1960 and 1990. Currently, the Interstate Highway System is 46,876 miles long.

In 1958, the Federal Aviation Agency (FAA) was authorized by the Federal Aviation Act to provide an independent agency to monitor and regulate the safe and efficient use of the national airspace. The Act transferred the Civil Aeronautics Authority's functions to a new independent FAA. The Department of Transportation (DOT) was created in 1967. It overlooks all forms of transportation including aviation. At that time, the Federal Aviation Agency was renamed the Federal Aviation Administration (FAA).

Alfred Kahn (an economist and deregulation advocate) became chairman of the Civil Aeronautics Board (CAB) in the mid-1970s. Around the same time, a British airline (Laker Airways) began offering inexpensive transatlantic flights. This awakened the need for U.S.-based airlines to lower their fares. At the time, the deregulation economic theory was taking root in the Republican Party. These influences led to Congress passing the Airline Deregulation Act of 1978. This Act ushered in an era of unencumbered free-market competition in the U.S. airline industry. The CAB was disbanded a few years thereafter.

Post-deregulation, new carriers entered the market and the big air carriers protected their markets with "hub" airports. Fares dropped as competition and the number of customers increased. A 1981 air-traffic-controllers strike brought a temporary setback to the growth. Some of the major carriers who had dominated the skies during the 1950s (such as Pan American and TWA) began to collapse in the wake of competition. These carriers disappeared completely following the first Gulf War and the subsequent recession of the early 1990s. By the late 1990s, the airlines that survived began enjoying record profitability.

In 2001, the airline industry had to deal with the effects of another economic downturn as business travel decreased substantially while labor and fuel costs increased. The events of 9/11 greatly magnified the airlines' issues. This led to a sharp decline in traffic and significantly higher operating costs. Losses continued for years. The industry didn't return to profitability until after consolidation had reduced the industry to just 4 major players—United, American, Delta and Southwest. This consolidation was completed by 2005.

A relatively stable period followed from 2005 to 2020. However, controversies arose over service quality, passenger treatment and flight delays. In 2010 and 2011, the U.S. Department of Transportation issued a series of rules that addressed these issues.

By the end of 2019, the major airlines were very profitable and they were growing. There were over 7,600 airliners flying 87,000 flights a day in the

U.S. The number of commercial airports in the U.S. had grown to over 500, and 926-million passengers flew domestically on the airlines that year.

In early 2020, the Covid-19 pandemic decimated business travel and the airlines were forced to drastically reduce the number of flights they were flying. On November 1, 2020, Transportation Security Administration (TSA) checkpoints cleared 936,092 passengers comparted to 2,459,525 on the same date in 2019.

In the early 1960s, America's communications infrastructure entered the digital age when research into what would become known as the "Internet" began. The Advanced Research Projects Agency Network (ARPANET) led to the development of protocols for "internetworking"–multiple separate networks joined together into a network of networks. The first 2 nodes of ARPANET were interconnected in 1969. Access to the ARPANET was expanded in 1981 when the National Science Foundation (NSF) developed the Computer Science Network (CSNET).

In 1982, the Internet Protocol Suite (TCP/IP) was standardized and the concept of a world-wide network of fully interconnected TCP/IP networks called the "Internet" was introduced. TCP/IP network access expanded again in 1986 when the National Science Foundation Network (NSFNET) provided access to supercomputer sites in the United States for research and education organizations.

Commercial internet service providers (ISPs) began to emerge in the late 1980s and early 1990s. The ARPANET was decommissioned in 1990. The Internet was commercialized in 1995 when NSFNET was decommissioned. That removed the last restrictions on the use of the Internet to carry commercial traffic. During the late 1990s, it was estimated that traffic on the public Internet grew by 100% per year, while the mean annual growth in the number of Internet users was between 20% and 50%. As of 2011, the estimated total number of Internet users was 2.1-billion (30.2% of the world's population). In 2019, close to 312-million internet users accessed the Web from the United States.

What to do about "infrastructure" "internal improvements" or "public works" has tormented America since its founding. Problems of infrastructure policy drove George Washington and others to form our constitutional system of government. In the Antebellum Era (1783 – 1864), South Carolina Congressman and Senator John C. Calhoun urged his fellow congressmen to "bind the Republic together with a perfect system of roads and canals." Of course, from the beginning the biggest problem with America's infrastructure development has been how to pay for it.

During the Great Depression (1929 – 1933) President Franklin Roosevelt proposed a public-works program "to put more men back to work, both directly on the public works themselves and indirectly in the industries supplying the materials for these public works," because "no country, however rich, can afford the waste of its human resources." Twenty years later, amid postwar peace and prosperity, President Eisenhower argued that "a modern, efficient highway system is essential to meet the needs of our growing population, our expanding economy and our national security."

Barack Obama, prior to his inauguration in 2009, promised Americans "shovel-ready projects all across the country." Infrastructure has always been seen as both a key to national prosperity and a fount of national anguish. Politicians have told us that infrastructure improvement will strengthen and perpetuate the Union, it will make us rich and it is the path to progress. Others have complained that it will bring us the pork barrel, it will cost us a fortune and it will ruin the environment.

For example, in a 2011 memorandum to the heads of the government's executive departments President Obama said, "To maintain our Nation's competitive edge, we must ensure that the United States has fast, reliable ways to move people, goods, energy, and information. In a global economy, where businesses are making investment choices between countries, we will compete for the world's investments based in part on the quality of our infrastructure."

President Obama also told the department heads that "investing in the Nation's infrastructure brings both immediate and long-term economic benefits—benefits that can accrue not only where the infrastructure is located, but also to communities all across the country. And at a time when job growth must be a top priority, well-targeted investment in infrastructure can be an engine of job creation and economic growth."

In 2009, the nation's debate over infrastructure improvements was fueled by the _Report Card for America's Infrastructure_. The report was released by the American Society of Civil Engineers (ASCE). The ASCE surveyed the nation's bridges, highways, dams, and levees. The ASCE concluded that "years of delayed maintenance and lack of modernization have left Americans with an outdated and failing infrastructure that cannot meet our needs." In the

ASCE's estimation, $2.2-trillion was needed to rehabilitate our infrastructure to a good condition within 5-years.

ASCE's conclusions have been resonating with Americans who have seen in recent years a surprising series of disastrous infrastructure failures. They include the Northeast electrical system blackout in 2003, the failure of the levees in New Orleans after Hurricane Katrina in 2005 and the Minneapolis I-35W bridge collapse in 2007.

And, America's infrastructure is all too often stressed far beyond its design limits. A good example of this is our nation's commercial airports. In 2019, an estimated 25% of airline-flight delays were caused by the lack of aviation infrastructure capacity. Today, America's infrastructure is what the Milken Institute Review calls "underinvested, unrepaired, outdated and outmoded."

Work: In colonial times, work was primarily farm-centric. Families were expected to be self-sufficient. They had to grow crops and raise livestock for their own consumption as well as for the few non-farmers in their communities. They also worked in "cottage industries" like soap and candle making.

Around the time of the First Continental Congress in 1774, a ship arrived from England with a cargo of indentured servants. This was how the early American labor market was supplied. This aspect of America's labor system was repugnant to the Founders.

The census of 1790 (the nation's first) tabulated a population of almost 4-million with only 202,000 living in towns with populations exceeding 2,500. American work was still based primarily on agriculture, but there were also jobs in the maritime industries, the small workshop industries and in highly-skilled crafts.

Planters in the South began raising tobacco, rice and indigo for export. Their vast plantations and the then-current cultivation practices required a large work force. Black slaves and indentured white workers provided the labor.

However, workers remained in short supply throughout the colonial period. To alleviate this problem, America adopted several forms of bound labor for white, European immigrants. It also accepted the coercive labor system for black Africans that had been established earlier. The free laborers were compensated with wages and free food and rum. Some worked in the nascent industries that used a "piece-work" wage system.

The American labor market was a "sellers' market" from the very beginning. Prevailing wages in the colonies and early America were relatively high. It was often heard that, "If the rate in wage increases continued, servants will be masters and masters will be servants."

England imposed the Sugar Act on America in 1764 and the Stamp Act in 1765. The Stamp Act was the first tax on American-produced-and-consumed products. These actions planted the seeds of America's labor movement. Many organizations were formed to protest the Acts with an emphasis on economic rather than political issues. Many of the members of these organizations were involved in pre-revolutionary agitation and became staunch patriots.

In the 1790s, labor and capital parted ways. A series of strikes signaled the beginning of the trade-union movement in America. It was focused on meeting the changing conditions of labor in the emerging industrial workplace.

In the 1800s, many Americans worked seventy hours or more per week and the length of the workweek became an important political issue. Typical jobs of the time were farmer, blacksmith, butcher, bricklayer, carpenter, clock smith, fisherman, barber, doctor, teacher, bookmaker, lawyer, coach driver and clerk. Men and women sometimes shared the same jobs.

The late 1800s and early 1900s saw a time of change, economic uncertainty and unrest in America. The growth of industrialism was largely unchecked after the Civil War. This created new jobs and new problems at the same time. Immigration was continuing in unprecedented numbers, especially from eastern and southern Europe. This forever altered the makeup of the American workforce.

A depression in 1893 (following 2 others in the previous 2 decades) forced some plants to close and many workers into the ranks of the unemployed. Labor-management disputes were widespread. Many of the workplace initiatives of today took root in this period. Women joined the workforce in increasing numbers. The number of white-collar and retail jobs grew rapidly. It became obvious that worker benefits, safe working conditions, reasonable work hours and vacations needed to be addressed.

In the 1890s, increasing numbers of Americans left their farms and took up urban industrial work. At that time, America boasted a variety of enterprises including the manufacture of iron, steel and textiles and the extraction and processing of crude oil. This trend marked a shift from a more agrarian way of life to that of labor for wages. Immigrants generally took factory jobs in the growing cities. These immigrant families and working-class Americans (including women and children) needed to work in the factories to survive.

The working conditions in factories were often harsh. Hours were long (typically 10-to-12 hours a day). Working conditions were frequently unsafe and led to deadly accidents. Tasks tended to be divided for efficiency's sake which led to repetitive and monotonous work for employees.

Dangerous-and-demeaning working conditions forced workers to organize. The American Federation of Labor (AFL) was founded in 1886. The Industrial Workers of the World (IWW) formed in 1905. In this period of labor unrest, many members in these unions (and others) were politically radical. They supported anarchism, communism and socialism as tools of change.

Strikes and boycotts were organized by these early labor groups to get management to negotiate for better working conditions and pay. However, they were rarely successful because management and the capitalists they worked for often asked the government for support to enforce their policies on workers. The Pullman Strike was one such instance where the government squelched a railway workers' strike by attaching mail cars to all the trains and then invoking the law that made it illegal to impede the movement of mail. There were many other, often deadly, confrontations between the establishment and workers.

The nascent labor movement caused Americans to see the excesses of the early capitalists and the need for reform. In the Progressive Era (1897 – 1920), reformers sought to improve the lot of the underprivileged by rectifying perceived wrongs.

President Theodore Roosevelt (1901 – 1909) supported the regulation of big business and often supported workers in their struggles to wrest a decent living from the industrialists. President Woodrow Wilson's (1913 – 1921) implemented Progressive principles with statutes that mandated an 8-hour workday for railroad workers, workers' compensation for injuries sustained on the job and the regulation of child labor.

In response to criticism, some companies instituted a "welfare capitalism" that provided employees with special benefits to secure their loyalty and to prevent unions from organizing their workforce. These benefits included subsidized housing, libraries and employee social clubs.

White-collar jobs grew rapidly because industrial capitalism led to the need for more administrative and clerical workers. These workers began to be classified as managers in the census as opposed to being classified with skilled craftsmen and unskilled labor.

The white-collar workers earned salaries instead of hourly wages or pay for piece-work. Social stratification began to emerge. It made white-collar jobs seem more desirable than blue-collar jobs. Children of immigrants aspired to such jobs to increase their social standing in a society that was often prejudiced against newcomers.

Work opportunities were limited for African-Americans. In the South, most were sharecroppers, agricultural wage laborers or small landowners. Others worked in industrial jobs, mining and forestry. African-American women frequently worked as domestic servants.

During World War I (1917 – 1918 for America), America's entire population and economy were mobilized to produce the personnel, food supplies, ammunition and money necessary to win the war. The government established multiple federal agencies to organize the necessary expertise to redirect the workforce from a peace to a war footing.

The American Federation of Labor (AFL) was a strong supporter of the war effort. Fear of disruptions to war production provided the AFL with political leverage that helped it gain recognition and negotiate favorable labor contracts. During the war, the AFL eschewed strikes and wages soared as near-full employment was reached at the height of the war. The Industrial Workers of the World (IWW) and radical socialists opposed the war.

The National War Labor Board was established in 1918 to keep factories running smoothly. It forced management to negotiate with labor unions. During WWI, AFL membership soared to 2.4-million. After the war, the AFL tried to solidify these gains by calling a series of major strikes in several industries. However, the strikes failed and membership and power declined.

The National Labor Relations Act of 1935 (aka the Wagner Bill) established a new national labor policy. The Act created a new independent agency—the National Labor Relations Board. The Act gave American workers the right to form and join unions. It also obligated employers to bargain collectively with employees in a "bargaining unit". The measure endorsed the principles of exclusive representation and majority rule, provided for enforcement of the Board's rulings and covered most workers in industries whose operations affected interstate commerce.

During World War II (1941 – 1945 for America) workers played a vital role in the production of war-related materials. Many of these workers were women. They began taking jobs in defense plants as welders, electricians, riveters, etc.

In addition to thousands of women entering the work force during the war, the American labor market changed radically in many other ways. The pressure of the need for national unity imposed a new dimension on race and labor conflicts. Tens-of-millions of workers moved from low-productivity to high-productivity and well-paying jobs. The workforce grew rapidly as students, retirees, housewives and the unemployed joined the active labor force. Work hours increased and time for leisure activities declined sharply.

When WWII ended in the summer of 1945, the U.S. economy faced an uncertain future. The unemployment rate had dropped to a record-low of 1.2% during the war (from 25% during the Great Depression and 14.6% in 1939), but with the end of the war millions of Americans who had been in uniform returned to the civilian workforce looking for jobs. And, it wasn't clear how well the economy would transition from a war footing to peacetime.

The worry was, however, unfounded. After the war, consumer demand grew rapidly and the military-industrial complex was gearing up for the Cold War. Prosperity gained ground rapidly. By 1950, the Gross Domestic Product of the United States and grown to $300-billion ($3.2-trillion in 2020 dollars). In 1960, it topped $500-billion ($4.4-trillion in 2020 dollars).

Organized labor had many reasons to be upbeat. Membership in the American Federation of Labor (AFL) and the Congress of Industrialized Organizations (CIO) at the end of WWII was 14.5-million. Union workers were 35% of America's workforce. Unions exercised this new power by calling for a series of strikes for better wages and working conditions. During the war, unions had agreed to not disrupt defense production with labor conflicts. But, after the war, they started to demand new-and-better labor contracts. Workers fought for increased wages, reasonable work hours and safer workplaces. The labor movement also led to efforts to stop child labor and to provide healthcare benefits to workers.

The GI Bill (a "workers" benefit for veterans) provided veterans with advanced education and vocational training. It also provided unemployment compensation and loans to veterans to purchase homes and start businesses. By the time the original GI Bill ended in 1956, 7.8-million (out of 16-million) World War II veterans had participated in the educational-and-training aspects of the program. And, from 1944 to 1952 the Veterans Administration backed nearly 2.4-million home loans for World War II veterans.

On the other hand, the Labor Management Relations Act of 1947 (aka the Taft–Hartley Act) was enacted to restrict the activities and power of labor unions. Even though it maintained various aspects of the National Labor Relations Act of 1935, the Taft-Hartley Act prohibited some labor-union practices. For Example, it banned discrimination against non-union members by union hiring halls, and it forbade closed shops. A closed shop is an employer that hires only union members.

In 1950, the total number of jobs in the U.S. stood at 43.5-million. Major changes in the American work experience took place in the 1950s. Women now made up 32% of the U.S. workforce. There was a large increase in the number of African-American workers who entered office work. The income gap between African-American and White men was reduced by about one-third. Offices acquired a "factory-floor" feel with rows of desks, bright overhead lighting and break rooms. And, just like in factories, the bosses had private corner offices with windows overlooking the "work floor" to make sure everyone was hard at work.

Those of us who entered the workforce in the 1960s (Boomers) found a work culture that was accurately depicted in the hit TV series "Mad Men". Drinking, smoking and not-politically-correct conversations were common. International Business Machines (IBM) introduced to the workplace machines that significantly improved worker productivity—the Selectric Typewriter (IBM 100) and business-computer systems.

Science fiction was a popular genre in the 1960s. In 1964, the famous science-fiction writer Arthur C. Clarke (2001: A Space Odyssey—1968) predicted the use of wireless communications, robotic surgery and the development of manned spaceflight. However, automakers and companies that produced oil and gas were still among the top-10 corporations in America. And, the Vietnam war was raging by the second half of the decade.

In 1970, there were about 140-million Americans eligible for work. Of those, 78.5-million were employed. There were 4.4-million unemployed. The remaining 55-million were categorized as "not in the labor force". The revolutionary 1960s had changed attitudes about work. These attitudes took root and blossomed in the 1970s. Workers began to look to the private sector for economic solutions rather than the government.

Personal liberation and rebellion became the hallmarks of the 1970s. Shocking clothing, long hair and strong individualism became popular. Businesses enforced workplace dress codes to varying degrees. Gradually, often-ignored dress-code infractions eroded the sanctity of the corporations' top-down policies. The term "sexual harassment" entered the American workplace lexicon in 1974.

The Arab Oil Embargo of 1973 – 1974 caused a stock-market crash and a recession. The U.S. Bureau of Labor Statistics estimated that 2.3-million jobs were lost during the recession. This was a post-WWII record. Although the recession ended in March 1975, the unemployment rate did not peak for several months.

The 1970s also brought on a wave of industrial deregulation. It started with the transportation and telecommunications industries and spread from there. Deregulation made competition the #1 priority for American businesses. And, the preference for shareholder capitalism over stakeholder capitalism introduced by Milton Friedman took root in the late 1970s. These shifts would cause massive changes in how employers and employees related to each other.

The 1980s opened with 2 recessions in 3 years. The "Black Monday" stock-market crash happened in 1987. American workers and their unions started advocating for "work-life balance" and "wellness programs". Conglomerates dominated the market and junk-bond artists started buying up companies, firing employees and demanding wage-and-working-condition concessions. In 1982, AT&T was broken up into regional companies through an anti-trust suit.

Technology started to become essential to the workplace. Personal computers (PCs) started occupying office desks. In 1984, Apple introduced its Macintosh PC. The first URL was registered and the World Wide Web appeared in 1989.

By the mid-1980s, the deregulation of the airline industry began to have significant effects on its approximately half-million employees. Airline employees struck their carriers 17 times from 1978-1989, and several airlines failed. Airline employees saw major cuts in pay along with additional working hours and the degradation of employee benefits such as retirement and health insurance plans.

The woes experienced by airline employees in the 1980s were also felt by workers in many other American industries as deregulation and shareholder-capitalism spread rapidly. However, America finished the decade with 19-million more jobs, but most of those jobs were low-pay and without good benefits.

In the early 1990s, American workers were increasingly doubting the value of long-term loyalty to the companies they worked for. They felt that their jobs were prosaic and their bosses were incompetent and overbearing. As the *New York Times* reported, "Companies that fail to factor in quality-of-employee-life issues when imposing total quality management or 're-engineering' or any other of the competitiveness-enhancing, productivity-improving schemes now popular, may gain little but a view of the receding backs of their best people leaving for friendlier premises." In an attempt to ameliorate this problem, many companies introduced "Casual Fridays" while they continued to hack away at workers' compensation and working conditions.

Towards the end of the decade, dot-com businesses were growing rapidly. Big-tech IPOs included Yahoo and Netscape. The birth of Amazon and eBay ushered in a new era of e-commerce. Millions of employees moved to these new, leading-edge companies with their looser cultures, relatively high pay and startup excitement. Cell phones, email and personal-digital assistants were leading technologies. Walmart became the third-largest company in America. Only the industrial giants GM and Ford were bigger.

In 1994, the first smartphone was sold. It was a cellphone, pocket organizer, beeper, calculator, digital camera, recorder, music player and color TV all packaged into a light unit that fit in a person's hand. It soon began to change the work lives of many Americans. The dot-com bubble (aka the "dot-com boom", the "tech bubble" and the "Internet bubble") started to inflate in 1995. In 1998, Exxon and Mobil consummated a $74-billion merger. It was the largest corporate merger ever. By the end of the decade, ExxonMobil was #1 in the Fortune 500. Consolidation and layoffs ensued.

In the early 2000s, the dot-com bubble burst sending millions of Americans with a high-tech education to the unemployment lines. In the crash that followed the bust, the Nasdaq index (which had risen 5-fold between 1995 and 2000) dropped from a peak of 5,048.62 on March 10, 2000, to 1,139.90 on Oct 4, 2002—a 77% fall.

The spreading use of technology in the workplace began to affect low-wage, lower-education jobs despite the dot-com bust. Just as technology had reduced the number of jobs on factory floors, it now reduced the number of administrative and retail jobs. Employment opportunities increasingly required applicants to have higher-level social and analytical skills rather than traditional physical and manual skills. Employment rose faster in jobs calling for greater preparation through education, experience and/or other types of training. The share of American women over 16 in the labor force peaked in 2000.

In 2003, a video titled "The Office of Tomorrow" was released by the consulting firm Accenture. It revealed new technology that could continuously track employees using "geolocation". Today, this technology is fueling the debate about workers' rights and privacy. The debut of most of the tech giants of today took place in the early 2000s—Skype (2003), Google (2004), Gmail (2004), Facebook (2006), Twitter (2006) and YouTube (2006). This rise of the big tech companies fueled the need for highly-trained tech workers.

The Great Recession of 2008 – 2009 was hard on American businesses and workers. This global economic downturn devastated world financial markets as well as the banking and real estate industries. The crisis led to increases in home-mortgage foreclosures and it caused millions of people to lose their jobs, their homes and their life savings. In America, the unemployment rate rose to 10%. After nearly going out of business, General Motors fell out of its traditional #1 spot, down to #6 on the Fortune 500 list.

In the 2010s, the U.S. economy slowly recovered from the Great Recession. Increasing globalization and the loss of blue-collar jobs in the recession caused a shift from manufacturing to service jobs. The tech sector became a huge component of the U.S. economy.

A multi-generational workforce emerged with Baby Boomers, Gen-Xers, Gen-Yers and Millennials working together in most companies. American-born non-Hispanic whites accounted for about 60% of the labor force. The Hispanic share of the labor force was 17% and African American 12%. Foreign-born workers accounted for 17% of the U.S. labor force, with

Asian immigrants making up a significant portion. Walmart, with $514-billion in revenues, was closing in on the tech giants Apple and Amazon.

At the end of the 2010s, artificial intelligence (AI) was being applied to business solutions and it had begun connecting everything we do. Workplace productivity tools like Slack, Microsoft Teams, Jira and Google Docs surged in popularity. Mobile apps became the norm for business communications. The cloud enabled workers to store and access huge amounts of data online from their PCs and mobile devices. It is predicted that AI and robotics will create more jobs than they destroy if we are smart in how we deploy and use them. It was predicted that most of the American workforce will be gig (freelance) workers by 2027. The pandemic seems to be accelerating this.

The rapid rate of change in the U.S. workforce and the nature of work show no signs of abating in 2020 despite the Covid-19 pandemic with its resulting economic downturn. In fact, the pandemic has accelerated the trends towards remote working and workplace automation.

The movement for a better work-life balance that started in the 1980s is continuing in 2020. Workers care less about where they work and more about how they work. Seventy-percent of high-performing teams believe the development of strong relationships with their team members is more important than individualism in the workplace. In this rapidly-changing world, transparency and information sharing are unleashing the potential of market leaders. Eighty-nine-percent of employees say that transparent decision making boosts team achievement.

The products and services that will win the hearts of customers will be the ones that are created by diverse teams that harness the varied perspectives of their members and share their ideas openly. Sixty-seven-percent of the high-achieving teams practice giving feedback to each other to strengthen their work and to produce better results. The future of work is evolving more rapidly than ever.

The future of work is being talked about because there are already too few jobs available for the number of people who need them. AI, robotics and automation will exacerbate this problem as we move forward. Deindustrialization, depressed investment and resistance from the Oligarchs are accelerating the trend towards fewer traditional jobs. Widespread job insecurity, jobless recoveries and stagnant wages are manifestations of this trend.

The political phenomena of continually-rising income-and-wealth inequality, populism and plutocracy also fuel this trend. The Oligarchs are more focused on building their moated castles and escaping to Mars than on improving the lives of the rest of us. A clear example of this is the highly-automated Tesla plant located just a few miles from the jobless masses in Oakland, CA.

There is little doubt that we need to change how we think about and adapt to the automated future that is rapidly approaching. This new future can easily be a disaster for most Americans due to massive technological unemployment, or it can provide us with the dream of freedom from toil.

To realize this dream, we must change how people secure the income they need to survive and prosper. Economists and others are talking about guaranteed incomes as a solution to the problem. *The Cornucopia Proposals* offer a more-comprehensive solution.

Chapter 3

Where We Want to Go

"Success is not the key to happiness. Happiness in the key to success.
  ~ Albert Schweitzer
    Physician, Writer, Philosopher, Theologian, Humanitarian

Now that we've clarified our current situation and reviewed how we got here, the next step in our situational-awareness process is to decide where we want to go. In my opinion, the destination we should all be happy to travel to is an America where <u>everyone</u> can enjoy the unalienable rights of Life, Liberty and the Pursuit (practice) of Happiness.

America's Founders declared in the U.S. Declaration of Independence:

> *That whenever any Form of Government becomes destructive*
> *of these ends, it is the Right of the People to alter or to*
> *abolish it, and to institute new Government, laying*
> *its foundation on such principles and organizing its powers in*
> *such form, as to them shall seem most likely to effect their*
> *Safety and Happiness."*

As I think you will agree, our current government is not delivering (to at least 95% of us) on the promise of Life, Liberty and the Pursuit of Happiness as the Founders intended. We now have the opportunity and obligation, almost 250-years later, to make Life, Liberty and the Pursuit of Happiness available to every American citizen. And, as you will see, we don't have to abolish our government. We only have to alter it a little to get us to our chosen destination.

To more clearly define our destination, let's start with getting on the same page about what happiness is. <u>Maslow's Hierarchy of Human Needs</u> is a good framework for us to use in our discussion of happiness.

American psychologist Abraham Maslow (1908 – 1970) developed his hierarchy in the 1940s. In the decades since then, an untold number of psychologist, psychiatrists, behaviorists and social scientists have expressed their alignment with Maslow's thinking. Most agree that if one achieves the pinnacle of Maslow's hierarchy (it's usually portrayed graphically as a pyramid), one can achieve happiness.

The 5 levels of Maslow's Hierarchy of Needs (from the base to the pinnacle) are:

1. Physiological Needs.
2. Safety Needs.
3. Social Needs.
4. Esteem Needs.
5. Self-Actualization Needs.

The first 2 needs, Physiological and Safety, are generally considered to be "Basic Needs". The next 2 needs, Social and Esteem, are called "Psychological Needs". The needs at the top of the pyramid are referred to as "Self- Actualization Needs". Maslow believed that fulfilling Self-Actualization Needs is contingent upon the lower-level needs being met first.

Let's take a closer look at each of the human needs in Maslow's hierarchy:

1. *Physiological Needs* are the basic requirements of human survival. They include air, food, drink, shelter, clothing, warmth, sex and sleep. In my opinion, in our modern society our needs for transportation and communications are also among our Physiological Needs. Maslow considered physiological needs the most important because all the other needs become secondary until Physiological Needs are met.

2. *Safety Needs* represent the second tier in Maslow's hierarchy. These needs include security of body, employment, resources, morality, family and health. The acquisition of our Safety Needs is obviously closely linked with our Physiological Needs.

3. *Social Needs* include love, acceptance and belonging. Some of the things that satisfy these needs include friendships, romantic attachments, family, social groups, community groups, professional

groups and churches.

4. *Esteem Needs* comprise self-confidence, strength, belief in oneself, personal acceptance, social approval, recognition and respect from others.

5. *Self-Actualization Needs* are basic to every human being. They are what drives us to realize our true potential and achieve our "ideal self". Self-actualization is achieved through creative growth, fulfilment and reaching our full potential. Obviously, to achieve self-actualization we must satisfy our physiological, safety, social and esteem needs first.

Here's what I think it will take to fulfill these needs for every American:

1. *Physiological Needs:* Based on my experience, research and calculations, I think in America today a job that pays an annual individual net income of $100,000 will provide an adult individual with the resources to satisfy her/his Physiological Needs. If 2 people decide to form a household, the combined basic income of $200,000 per year should provide these physiological needs for all the members of the household (including children).

2. *Safety Needs:* A guaranteed basic annual income of $100,000 will also provide the resources that are required for safety and security. Guaranteed employment for everyone over the age of 18, and a few modifications to how we structure work, will take care of the need for employment security. The morality that is practiced in our society needs to evolve to where individual physical security is at the top of our priority list and the sanctity of the common good is placed ahead of the worship of the individual and money. Good health comes from healthy habits and excellent healthcare. Education, training and incentives can change the way Americans take care of themselves. Healthcare for all that achieves outstanding outcomes will ensure good health and continue to increase our lifespans.

3. *Social Needs*: The resources that are needed to find and maintain friendships, romantic attachments, family ties and group memberships are readily available in the United States now. I believe that to fulfill the needs at this level for all Americans we must tweak our culture to include formal and practical education, training and guidance on how to seek, identify, capture and maintain our

relationships with other human beings. A reasonable work-life balance is also needed. Of course, Physiological and Safety Needs will also have to be met to enable one to satisfy his/her Social Needs.

4. *Esteem Needs:* There are many available avenues to achieving self-confidence, strength, belief in oneself, personal acceptance, social approval, recognition and respect from others once one's Physiological, Safety and Social Needs are met. With an individual income of at least $100,000 per year and a restructuring of work in America, people will have the time and money that it takes to satisfy these Esteem Needs. If formal, practical and on-going education, training and guidance is available, I believe every American will be able to satisfy their Esteem Needs.

5. *Self-Actualization Needs:* When Physiological, Safety, Social and Esteem Needs are met, everyone will have the opportunity and the resources needed to achieve their true potential through creative growth. Creative growth requires a plan, time, resources and guidance. The elements that are needed for creative growth will be available to every American through programs that are part of their guaranteed basic annual compensation package.

The America described above starts with every American 18-and-over having a guaranteed job that pays at least $100,000 per year. I can think of several ways that we could do this. Let's look at one of them.

Imagine that we have an *"American Contribution Corps"* (ACC). Any American citizen 18-years of age or older is guaranteed employment by the ACC. Employees of the ACC, known as "Corps members", must qualify for service in the Corps through preparatory education and training, aptitude screening and knowledge-and-skills testing appropriate to the contributions to the common good they want to make.

American Contribution Corps (ACC) employment benefits include:

1. A starting annual salary of $100,000 (net).
2. An annual cost-of-living salary increase equal to the rate of inflation in the prior year.
3. Performance bonuses.

4. ACC-paid preparatory, initial and recurrent training required for employment by the ACC.
5. ACC-paid health-insurance coverage equal to, or better than, Medicare/Medicare-Advantage.
6. Thirty-days paid vacation per year.
7. Paid family and sick leave.
8. The freedom and time to pursue activities to generate additional income and/or to pursue creative growth.

American Contribution Corps (ACC) employment obligations include:

1. Corp members must use their best efforts to contribute to the common good through assignments to ACC programs, projects and task forces.
2. Corp members must provide 1,040 hours per year (avg. 20-hours per week) of work on assigned ACC-approved work (including training time).
3. Corp members must complete ACC initial and recurrent training as assigned.
4. Corp members must adhere to the ACC code of conduct and all other policies and procedures adopted by the ACC.

How would this work in practice? Again, there are several ways to structure the ACC. One of the ways I can envision that would work is illustrated in the following scenarios.

Scenario 1: The New High School Graduate

A newly graduated 18-year-old woman (let's call her Jill) is ready to take her place as a contributor to the common good. Jill's K-12 education and training has prepared her to function in our modern society. She is proficient in learning, math, science, technology, interpersonal communications, teamwork, problem solving, critical thinking and the creative process.

At this point, Jill is not sure what her life's mission will be. She's interested in a lot of things and she's anxious to start living an "adult" life by contributing to the common good. But, she's not ready to commit to a definite career path.

In her high-school senior year, Jill went through the *American Contribution Corps* (ACC) pre-employment process and it has been determined that she is qualified for a job as a member of the Corps. Contributors can be assigned to any ACC-approved job that they are qualified for and capable of doing. These jobs range from manual-labor, sanitation, retail, fast food, etc. to highly-technical, scientific and leadership positions. If Jill isn't qualified for a job she'd like to do, the ACC will provide the education and training necessary for her to qualify for it.

Jill is interested in becoming a doctor, but she's not yet ready to make the commitment to the education and training that will be required for her to qualify for that profession. So, she wants to dip her toe in the water by working as a hospital medical assistant. The ACC provides the training Jill needs and then assigns her to a hospital with an opening in that position. Based on the training required for that position, Jill must make a 2-year commitment to the job. Her starting annual salary is $100,000 (net) and she must work 20-hours per week to earn that pay. Jill has the option to work additional hours at a rate of pay she can negotiate with the hospital.

Jill can use her considerable "free" time to pursue other interests, continue her education towards her goal of becoming a doctor or anything else she cares to do with her time. After 6 months in the medical-assistant role, Jill decides that she wants to become a doctor. Her training and experience as a medical assistant make it easy for her to pass her qualifying exams for medical school.

She spends the next 6 years pursuing her goal of becoming a doctor. The ACC pays for her medical-school and training costs. Because she is putting in at least 20-hours per week on this ACC-required training, the ACC is paying her $100,000 per year. That provides Jill with a decent standard of living while she is in school/training. Jill was required to commit to practicing medicine for a minimum of 10 years after she receives her doctor's license.

After Jill completes her training to be a doctor, she decides to set up her own practice. The money she needs for facilities, equipment, etc. is provided by the ACC. Jill is paid $8,333 per month ($100,000 per year/12 months) by the ACC for the first 20 hours she works at her practice each week because the

ACC considers the provision of medical services to be in the common good. Jill is also free to charge whatever the market will bear for her services.

If Jill meets her ACC-employment obligations, she will receive her $100,000 per year (plus cost-of-living increases) in addition to what she earns from her practice. When Jill reaches the minimum retirement age of 70, she can retire at any time. If she chooses to put in at least 5-hours per week working for the Corps on common-good projects, she will receive $100,000 per year plus other ACC-provided benefits. If she decides to completely retire, she will receive an annual retirement benefit of $50,000 plus health insurance coverage. Jill can still enjoy the income and benefits she receives from her medical practice in addition to her ACC retirement benefits.

Scenario 2: The New College Graduate

Dan, who just completed his bachelor's degree in robotic engineering, has secured a position as an entry-level engineer in a leading-edge robotics startup. He has been an employee of the *American Contribution Corps* (ACC) since he graduated from high school at age 18. Throughout college, Dan received $100,000 per year plus benefits since he was in an ACC-approved education program. This paid for his living expenses. His college costs (tuition, books, fees, etc.) were paid by the ACC.

Dan has committed to work a minimum of 20-hours per week as a robotics engineer for the startup. He had to commit to working as a robotics engineer for a minimum of 5 years due to the length and complexity of his education/training. Because he was caught up in the excitement of participating in the building of a new company, he has been working an additional 20-hours per week for additional compensation that he worked out with the company.

For the rest of his career as a robotics engineer, Dan continues to meet his ACC-employment obligations. So, he will receive his $100,000 per year (plus cost-of-living increases and benefits) in addition to what he earns in his spare time.

When Dan reaches the minimum retirement age of 70, he can retire at any time. If he chooses to put in at least 5-hours per week working for the Corps on common-good projects, he will receive $100,000 per year plus other ACC-provided benefits. If he decides to completely retire, he will receive an annual retirement benefit of $50,000 plus health insurance coverage.

Scenario 3: Mid-Career Change

Marybeth is 44. She graduated from college with a bachelor's degree in computer science and a master's degree in business 15-years ago. Like Dan, she has been an employee of the *American Contribution Corps* (ACC) since high school graduation. Throughout college, she received $100,000 per year since she was in an ACC-approved education program. This paid for her living expenses. Her college costs (tuition, books, fees, etc.) were paid by the ACC.

Upon graduation, the Corps placed her in a full-time position (20-hours per week) with a large computer-services-consulting firm in her home town. She has been working there as a computer programmer and, for the past 5-years, as a team leader. She has been paid $100,000 per year by the ACC for her job at the consulting company. In her spare time, Marybeth started a small business and has been earning additional income from this venture. As a result, she's been living a comfortable-and-secure lifestyle and she's been able to save a considerable amount for retirement and for other opportunities she may want to take advantage of.

However, Marybeth is having a mid-life crisis. In recent years, she's felt stifled by working in a large organization and she's been thinking about how she would prefer to be a bigger fish in a smaller pond. She wants to strike out on her own and start a computer-services-consulting company. Conserving her savings and maintaining her steady income are part of the startup plan she and her advisors have been developing for a couple of years.

The first step in executing the plan is to gain designation from the ACC for the new business as a "common-good" business. The ACC grants this designation to startup organizations, both for-profit and not-for-profit, with business plans that show how the organization is going to contribute to the common good.

With this designation, Marybeth will continue to receive her $100,000-per-year income as long as she puts in at least 20-hours per week working for the new company. Another benefit from the designation is that the startup capital that Marybeth needs to setup, staff, equip and run the new company until it breaks even will be provided by the ACC in the form of an unsecured convertible note. She can pay off the note with profits from her consulting company, her savings and/or by bringing in investors. If she decides not to pay off the note, the ACC will convert the note into equity in the company.

When Marybeth reaches the minimum retirement age of 70, she can retire at any time. If she chooses to put in at least 5-hours per week working for the Corps on common-good projects, she will receive $100,000 per year plus other ACC-provided benefits. If she decides to completely retire, she will receive an annual retirement benefit of $50,000 plus health insurance coverage. Marybeth can still enjoy the income and benefits she receives from her company in addition to her ACC retirement benefits.

Scenario 4: The New Parents

Sue and Bill have been living together for the past 3-years. They are both 33-years old and they've decided it's time to start a family. Since they've been members of the *American Contribution Corps* (ACC) since they turned 18, they have been living very-comfortable lifestyles on their $100,000 individual incomes. When they started living together, they decided to equally share household costs. Their combined $200,000 annual income has allowed them to live very comfortably and to have plenty of disposable income. And, they've both managed to put away a considerable nest egg.

They are planning on purchasing a house to start their new family in. So, they'll use part of their savings for the down payment and they'll continue to work 20-hours per week at ACC-assigned jobs so that their combined income will qualify them for the mortgage they will need. They will receive 6-months of fully-paid parental leave when each of their new babies arrives. They can take the leave sequentially so one of them can provide full-time parenting at a time—a combined 1-year of full-time parenting—while maintaining their $200,000 combined annual income. And, of course, the 20-hours-per-week they are required to put in on ACC work leaves them with considerable available parenting time. And, the ACC will pay for any needed child care that may be required.

Sue and Bill plan on having 3 children spaced 3-years apart. Their ACC-paid-for health insurance will cover the costs of the births and the children's healthcare until they reach the age of 18. The children's primary education-and-training will also be paid for by the government through the public-school system.

If the children decide to join the ACC when they turn 18, their secondary education/training costs will be covered by the ACC and they will earn $100,000 (plus benefits) per year if the education/training programs are approved by the ACC.

When Sue and Bill reach the minimum retirement age of 70, they can retire at any time. If they choose to put in at least 5-hours per week working for the Corps on common-good projects, they will each receive $100,000 per year plus other ACC-provided benefits. If they decide to completely retire, they will each receive an annual retirement benefit of $50,000 plus health insurance coverage.

Scenario 5: The Vagabond

Mark just graduated from high school with a major case of wanderlust. He has no clear career goal, but he's been planning for some time on "seeing the world" before he starts a career. Mark has been accepted for the *American Contribution Corps* (ACC) "Global-Development Program". The program provides personnel and funding for ACC projects around the world that contribute to America's common good. These projects include outreach, community-development and research projects that create and maintain positive links between Americans and citizens of other countries.

His participation in the Global-Development Program requires Mark to put in at least 10-hours per week on a ACC-approved project as he's traveling the world. For that contribution, he will receive an annual income of $50,000, full healthcare coverage, travel-expense coverage and ACC-paid education/training. Mark must serve in the program for at least 6-months at a time. He can remain in the program for a total of 3-years. He's planning on spending most of the next 3-years abroad working on Global-Development Program projects in Europe, Africa, the Middle East and South America.

When he leaves the Global-Development Program, Mark will be obligated to serve in an ACC-assigned "Basic Infrastructure" job for 1-year for each year he served in the program. Basic Infrastructure jobs include fast-food service, sanitation, construction, retail and maintenance positions. Mark will be required to put in 20-hours per week on these jobs. For that contribution, he will receive a salary of $100,000 per year plus healthcare, sick-leave, vacation, retirement and education/training benefits.

When Mark reaches the minimum retirement age of 70, he can retire at any time. If he chooses to put in at least 5-hours per week working for the Corps on common-good projects, he will receive $100,000 per year plus other ACC-provided benefits. If he decides to completely retire, he will receive an annual retirement benefit of $50,000 plus health insurance coverage.

Scenario 6: The Retiree

Kurt is 73-years old. He worked for the largest airline in the world for over 22-years. He took an early retirement when he was 42 to pursue his entrepreneurial dreams. The retirement benefits he earned with the airline were supposed to provide him with approximately $15,000 per month, fully-paid healthcare and free airline-travel when he turned 60.

Unfortunately, the owners of the airline employed a strategy that has become popular in America since the early 1980s. They bankrupted the company (just before Kurt turned 60) and handed the severally underfunded company pension plan over to the government. The result of this maneuver was the reduction of Kurt's retirement benefit to under $1,000 per month. And, the company-paid-for health insurance and free travel never materialized. Kurt has been supporting himself and his wife by working as a management consultant since his retirement income doesn't cover his living expenses.

Due to deteriorating health and the vicissitudes of life, Kurt would like to retire, but his retirement and social-security income total under $30,000 per year. Living modestly but comfortably costs him over $80,000 per year. He's worried he won't be able to continue to secure consulting gigs much longer. On the other hand, he wants to maintain a modest work load to keep his mind sharp.

So, Kurt joined the *American Contribution Corps* (ACC). He's putting in 20-hours per week on ACC-assigned projects like consulting to startup companies and contributing his aviation expertise to the ACC Aviation Industry Task Force. He's earning $100,000 per year plus other ACC-provided benefits. Since Kurt is already past the minimum retirement age of 70, he can retire at any time. If he chooses to put in at least 5-hours per week working for the Corps on common-good projects, he will receive $100,000 per year plus other ACC-provided benefits. If he decides to completely retire, he will receive and annual retirement benefit of $50,000 plus health insurance coverage.

Working for the *American Contribution Corps* (ACC) provides members of the Corps with the resources they need to satisfy their Basic Needs (Physiological and Safety)—money and time. To secure their Psychological (Social and Esteem) and Self-Actualization Needs, Corps members will also need a rational "Life Plan".

Corps members receive education, training and guidance on creating and maintaining their personal Life Plan. This begins with their 8-week basic training program and continues throughout their career with the Corps. They're provided with assessment and self-discovery tools to help them in creating their Life Plan. And, the Corps provides them with access to a team of life coaches. Of course, the Life Plan will be a living document with many twists and turns throughout the Corps-member's lifetime.

I believe that *American Contribution Corps* members will therefore be practicing happiness throughout their lives because their Maslow's-Hierarchy Needs are being satisfied. This will make them more-productive citizens and lessen many of the tensions currently extant in our country. I can also envision the virtual elimination of poverty, violent crime, ignorance, racism, science denial, anti-social drug addiction and anti-common-good behavior.

Among the projects and programs the *American Contribution Corps* (ACC) sponsors are "Task Forces" that are working on the elimination of poverty, hunger and inequality; the eradication of life-threatening diseases; the achievement of peaceful worldwide coexistence and the abolition of war; the design and implementation of climate-change-mitigation strategies; the protection of the biosphere; infrastructure improvement; healthcare advancement; lifespan extension; universal, free education and training; the elimination of violent behavior; rationalizing and updating our economic and political systems; and many others that contribute to the common good. Participation in these Task Forces provides Corps members with the Esteem and Self-Actualization Needs that are required for happiness while massively contributing to the common good.

Imagine the results that will be yielded by focusing educated, trained, highly-motivated and happy Americans on solving the existential problems that we face. Human beings are above all else problem solvers. And, we have plenty of problems to be solved if the human race is to survive. When the brain power of millions of *American Contribution Corps* members is brought to bear on solving these and future problems, I'm confident the hands of the Doomsday Clock that is maintained by the *Bulletin of the Atomic Scientists* will be moved back to a much-more encouraging position.

American businesses from startups to established large corporations and not-for-profits will significantly benefit from the *American Contribution Corps* (ACC) labor force. Any American organization that produces products and/or services that contribute to the common good (as determined by the ACC) can requisition ACC-employed workers. Corps members who are assigned to these approved organizations are paid by the ACC for the first 20-hours per week they work for the approved organization. The assigned workers' healthcare, sick-leave, family-leave, education/training and retirement benefits are also paid for by the ACC. If an approved organization wants to employ an assigned worker for more than 20-hours per week, and the assigned worker consents to working the additional hours, the approved organization compensates the assigned worker for the additional work at a rate that is negotiated by the worker and approved organization.

The Corps members who are assigned to ACC-approved organizations are fully qualified for the assigned work. This eliminates training costs for the approved organization and increases the organization's efficiency since workers are fully qualified for the job before they start working for the organization. Recurrent training is also paid for by the ACC. Corps members are obligated to work for the approved organization for a minimum period that is based on the cost of initial and recurrent training for the position filled.

One or two Corps members can cover a 40-hours-per-week position for an approved organization. If one Corps member works the 40-hours-per-week position, the ACC pays the Corps member for the first 20-hours per week worked (plus benefits) and the approved organization compensates the Corps member for the second 20-hours per week (plus overtime pay for working more than 40-hours per week). Approved organizations may opt to requisition two Corps members to fill one 40-hour-per-week position (20-hours per week each). In this case, the approved organization is enjoying the benefits of a free workforce.

The *American Contribution Corps* (ACC) is only one way we can redirect our country from the verge of civil war and economic collapse to a future of solid progress, equality and happiness. However, there are many ways to peel an onion. If you have a better idea than the ACC, please get it into the mix of ideas that are currently circulating.

The important thing is that we recognize that we can create a viable way out of our current dilemma by taking advantage of a rare situation that makes significant change possible. And, imagine what it will be like living in a country were all its citizens are practicing their unalienable right to be happy, not just a 5% segment of our society.

Chapter 4

How We're Going to Get There

"We cannot solve our problems with the same thinking we used when we created them."
    ~ Albert Einstein
      Theoretical Physicist (1879 – 1955)

"Destiny is not fate, it's navigation."
    ~ Richie Norton
      "The Power of Starting"

Now that we've selected our destination—***an America where every citizen has the resources and opportunities he/she needs for the practice of happiness***—we need to create a vehicle to get us there. My vehicle of choice is built upon *The Cornucopia Proposals*.

    Proposal 1: The Congress shall enact the *American Contribution Act of 2021*.

    Proposal 2: The Act shall establish the *American Contribution Administration* (ACA).

    Proposal 3: The ACA shall establish the *American Contribution Corps* (ACC).

    Proposal 4: The Congress shall establish the *American Contribution Trust Fund* (ACTF).

    Proposal 5: The Congress shall establish the *American Common Good Fund* (ACGF).

    Proposal 6: The Congress shall establish the *American Cornucopia Fund* (ACF).

The first step in building our transportation vehicle is for the U.S. Congress to pass the ***American Contribution Act of 2021***. The new Act will establish a new Administration—the ***American Contribution Administration*** (ACA).

Establishing an Administration at the Federal level to address the needs of American citizens has been common in our history. For example, the Drug Enforcement Administration (DEA) was established in 1973, the National Oceanic and Atmospheric Administration (NOAA) in 1970, the Federal Aviation Administration (FAA) and the National Aeronautics and Space Administration (NASA) in 1958, the Small Business Administration (SBA) in 1953, the Social Security Administration (SSA) and the Work Projects Administration (WPA) in 1935, the Federal Housing Administration (FHA) in 1934 and the Civilian Conservation Administration (CCA) in 1933 (The CCA was superseded by Civilian Conservation Corps in 1937).

The *American Contribution Administration* (ACA) will be responsible for administering all congressionally-authorized policies and programs related to the contributions of American citizens to the common good of our country. Its budget will be funded by the U.S. Treasury with funds provided by the Federal Reserve Bank of USA. The ACA will be headed by an Administrator who is appointed by the President and confirmed by the Senate.

American Contribution Administration (ACA) programs will include:

1. Moonshot Programs:
    a. Cure for diseases and afflictions like Covid-19, cancer, ALS, heart disease, stroke, etc.
    b. Environmental protection.
    c. Climate-change mitigation.
    d. Quality-of-life, healthcare and life-span improvements.
    e. Settlement of the Moon and Mars.
    f. Global demilitarization.
    g. Equalization of rights and justice.
    h. Development of robotics and artificial intelligence for the automation of blue-collar jobs.

2. Infrastructure Programs:
    a. Upgrades and maintenance.
    b. Universal internet and cellphone access.
    c. Transition to clean energy.
    d. New and/or improved transportation systems.
3. Societal Programs:
    a. The elimination of poverty.
    b. A significant reduction in violent crime.
    c. Education and training.
    d. Universal healthcare.
4. Economic Programs:
    a. Economic expansion.
    b. Business development.
    c. Elimination of personal and corporate income tax.

Personnel for *American Contribution Administration* (ACA) programs will be provided by the *American Contribution Corps* (ACC). The ACC will be funded and managed by the ACA.

Any American citizen 18-years of age or older is guaranteed employment by the ACC. Employees of the ACC, known as "Corps Members", must qualify for service through preparatory education and training, aptitude-screening and knowledge-testing appropriate to the contributions they will be making to the common good through ACA programs. Details of the Corp Members' benefits and obligations can be found in Chapter 3.

The *American Contribution Administration* (ACA) will establish and administer an ***American Contribution Trust Fund*** (ACTF). The purpose of the ACTF will be to provide a trust fund for every American that will enable them to emerge into adulthood at age 18 with a "nest egg" that can help them to start investing in their future.

Upon a U.S. citizen's birth and on the anniversary of that birth through age 18, $20,000 will be credited to an ACTF-administered trust fund for that citizen—a total of $360,000 over 18 years. The funds thus deposited will be invested in government bonds that bear an appropriate rate of interest. With an assumed interest rate of 4%, the investment will yield $553,000 (principle and interest) at the 18th year.

Withdrawals from the citizen's ACTF trust fund may be made by the beneficiary after she/he reaches age 18. Up to 5% of the balance of the trust fund may be withdrawn each year for personal reasons. Any withdrawals in excess of 5% must be approved by the ACTF. Approved withdrawals may include capital to start a business or not-for-profit organization, an investment in a company that contributes to the common good and other activities that contribute to the common good. Any balance remaining in the citizen's individual trust fund when she/he dies will be returned to the U.S. Treasury. The ACTF will be funded by the *American Cornucopia Fund* (ACF).

The *American Contribution Administration* (ACA) will establish and administer an *American Common Good Fund* (ACGF). The ACGF will make grants to *American Contribution Corps* (ACC) members to fund programs, projects, businesses and organizations that have received ACA approval. ACA approval will be based on the merits of submitted plans as they relate to the common good.

These proposals, if adopted, could solve most of the existential societal problems we're currently facing. They can dramatically rebalance the inequality that 95% of Americans are suffering from. And, it can focus the talents and brainpower of tens-of-millions of Americans on solving the problems that are now threatening to destroy the American Dream. But, how the heck are we going to pay for all this? That's a fair question. There is more than one answer, but let's look at one way I can think of to answer it.

The *American Contribution Act of 2021* will also provide for setting up and funding the ***American Cornucopia Fund*** (ACF). The ACF will provide funding for the *American Contribution Administration* (ACA), the *American Contribution Trust Fund* (ACTF) and the *American Common Good Fund* (ACGF).

I'm sure you're familiar with the first definition of "cornucopia", but in fact there is more than one meaning. The one you're probably thinking of is "a curved, hollow goat's horn or similarly shaped receptacle (such as a horn-shaped basket) that is overflowing with fruit and vegetables". This definition is usually portrayed as a <u>decorative motif emblematic of abundance</u>. The second definition is more applicable to our discussion—***an inexhaustible store; abundance.*** Related synonyms include "gold mine", mother lode", "treasure trove" and "wellspring".

Virtually every American citizen who has ever lived has contributed, in one way or another, to accumulating the knowledge and resources needed to make the *American Cornucopia Fund* (ACF) a reality. Their intelligence, hard work, sacrifices and creativity—applied in the pursuit of prosperity, security, growth and wealth—has given us a solid and prospering capitalism, a democracy that provides the needed mechanisms for change and an unlimited supply of U.S. Dollars. Let's take a closer look at each of these enablers.

Capitalism: Ever since the American colonists brought capitalism with them from England, it has been evolving. Our American form of capitalism has enabled our country of primarily poor immigrants to attain dominion over a vast continent, a top-tier standard of living and leadership of the Free World.

However, it is vitally important to understand that capitalism is not a natural phenomenon or force of nature. It was created by people and it has been modified an untold number of times by people. In her book "The Relentless Revolution: A History of Capitalism" (Norton), Joyce Appleby (American historian, 1929 – 2016) points out that "Capitalism is not a unified, coordinated system. Rather it is a set of practices and institutions that permit billions of people to pursue their economic interests in the marketplace."

We must also keep in mind that there are many different "flavors" of capitalism. We're all familiar with the current U.S. shareholder capitalism. However, the Chinese practice a distinctly different form of capitalism as do the Russians. The European form of capitalism is much like that of the U.S., but there are important differences. And, the "flavor" of U.S. capitalism has changed continuously over the years. Over the past 100-years or so, it has swung from shareholder capitalism to stakeholder capitalism and back to its current resting point of shareholder capitalism.

I launched my first entrepreneurial venture in 1959 at the age of 12 by establishing a paper route for the Chicago Tribune. I was living in a new post-World War II "instant subdivision" west of Chicago, IL. As it happened, there was no *Chicago Tribune* paper route in my neighborhood yet. I had to sign my neighbors up for subscriptions, deliver their paper every day and then collect their subscription fees at the end of every month—basic entrepreneurship. Eight years later (1967), I launched my second entrepreneurial venture (an air-charter company) and then spent the next 22 years working for one of the largest corporations on the planet (United Airlines) while founding other intrapreneurial (United) and entrepreneurial (outside) ventures.

The flavor of capitalism that was favored in America when I started making my way in the economy was what Robert B. Reich in his excellent and enlightening book "The System: Who Rigged It, How We Can Fix It" (Penguin Random House, 2020) calls *"Stakeholder Capitalism"* (as opposed to "Shareholder Capitalism"). The directors and CEOs of companies who were practicing Stakeholder Capitalism at that time (1960s)—and most of them were—had an ethical, moral and legal mandate to balance the interests of their customers, employees, suppliers, shareholders and their local and national communities. Under this system, a company's purpose is to create long-term value and not to maximize short-term profits and enhance shareholder value at the expense of other stakeholder groups.

I believe that serving the interests of all stakeholders (as opposed to only shareholders) is essential to the long-term success of any business and of our country. It is the sensible business decision and the right ethical-and-moral choice. I worked and flourished in this Stakeholder-Capitalism environment at United Airlines (as an employee and intrapreneur) and in my independent businesses (as a shareholder). The U.S. economy thrived on this flavor of capitalism from roughly World War II to the early 1980s. I am a very-strong supporter of Stakeholder Capitalism.

However, in 1970 Milton Friedman (American economist 1912 – 2006) revealed his "Friedman Doctrine" in an essay for *The New York Times* titled "A Friedman Doctrine: The Social Responsibility of Business is to Increase Its Profits". This doctrine is also referred to as "shareholder theory" and "stockholder theory". The Friedman Doctrine is a theory of business ethics which holds that a company's primary responsibility is to its shareholders and not its other constituents. *The New Economic Foundation* defines "Shareholder Capitalism" as "A system driven by the interests of shareholder-backed and market-fixated companies."

This shareholder primacy flavor of capitalism views shareholders as the driving economic force of the organization and the only group to which the firm is socially responsible. The goal of the company is to maximize returns to shareholders. Friedman argued in his article that the shareholders can then decide for themselves what social initiatives to take part in.

We are now witnessing how well that's worked out. The Oligarchs have benefited immensely from the wealth they have accumulated through shareholder capitalism. But the social initiatives they've backed with this rapidly increasing wealth have been focused on gutting the social safety net, decimating unions, holding real wages down for 95% of Americans and feathering their own nests at the expense of the rest of us.

From the mid-1970s through today, the Friedman Doctrine has been taught in virtually every business school in the U.S., and it has been adopted by most, if not all, of the corporations in America. In his 2017 Working Paper for the Minnesota Law Review titled "A Legal Theory of Shareholder Primacy", Robert J. Rhee states "Shareholder primacy is the most fundamental concept in corporate law and corporate governance."

For corporate CEOs and directors, it has become an obligation to the Oligarchs and a rule of law. Rhee states, "The rule does not exist in a single locus duty, but instead is a filamentary principle that weaves through many other rules of corporate law and the architecture of the corporate and market systems."

Shareholder Capitalism has been the guiding economic theory in the U.S. for approximately 40-years. It has worked well for shareholders who are in the top 5% of the income and wealth rankings in America. But, as we saw in Chapter 2 "How Goes It: How We Got Here", it has not done the same for the other 95% of Americans.

The Cornucopia Proposals advocates for a swing of the "Capitalism Pendulum" from the extreme form of shareholder capitalism that is now extant in America back towards the type of stakeholder capitalism that served most Americans well from the end of World War II to the late 1970s. This swing has, I believe, begun with the current push for a more-equitable society. Momentum can be added to the swing by a few changes to the norms, practices and laws that have crept into economic thinking over the past 5 decades and by adopting *The Cornucopia Proposals*.

One indication that the capitalism-pendulum is about to swing back towards stakeholder capitalism is the 2019 Business Roundtable pronouncement that American corporations should choose stakeholder capitalism over shareholder capitalism as their guiding business-model principle. The CEOs of 181 leading U.S. corporations signed the statement. However, to-date we've seen very little change in the behavior of these companies. If they truly want to see a swing back towards stakeholder capitalism, they will back the passage of the *American Contribution Act of 2021*.

It appears that although the pendulum is ready to swing, it needs a push from the 95% of the American electorate who will benefit most from the swing. Of course, the swing will begin much sooner if the Oligarchs would be so kind as to loosen their grip on it just a little. The push is currently being exerted by a sizable portion of Americans who are supporting the equality-for-all and human-rights movements. And, there are signs that the Oligarchs are at least open to discussing how the pendulum might swing back towards equilibrium.

Every American from the poor to the rich and everyone in between will benefit from the swing. Remember, all flavors of capitalism are the result of human choices. We can make the pendulum swing if we want to and if we act now. After all, an economy that serves all Americans is what the Founders had in mind when they wrote the U.S. Declaration of Independence and Constitution. No matter where the pendulum rests after this swing, American Capitalism can provide the means—financial and structural—to make the *American Contribution Administration* a reality.

Democracy: Like capitalism, democracy comes in many flavors. Most scholars consider America's flavor to be a "Democratic Republic". In this flavor, some decisions (usually local) are made by a direct democratic process, and other decisions (frequently at the federal level) are made by democratically-elected representatives, A Democratic Republic operates on principles adopted from republics and democracies.

The changes that are needed to make "happiness for all" a reality in America will be made to federal laws and regulations. Therefore, our U.S. Senators and Representatives will have to be convinced and motivated to pass legislation like the *American Contribution Act of 2021* that mandate the needed changes. Our Democratic Republic provides the mechanisms by which we can convince and motivate our elected representatives. But, some changes will be needed.

As has become abundantly obvious in recent years, our elected and appointed representatives are routinely forced to make decisions that are in the interests of roughly 5% of the population and not in the interests of the other 95%. I'm thinking of the rollbacks in environmental and climate-change laws and regulations, the gutting of the National Labor Relations Act, the repeal of the Glass-Steagall Act and the 2010 Supreme Court *Citizens United* decision to name a few.

We all know that our federal representatives must raise large campaign funds for each election they stand in. They need this money to create a grassroots organization, pay for political ads and fend off attacks by their opponents. Consequently, they go to where the money is—the top 5% income-earners. This group is made up of the Oligarchs and their underlings (bankers, lawyers, CEOs, etc.) who now control the U.S. economy and politics.

Only 9%-to-18% of political contributions come from the 95% of Americans who make less than $100,000 per year. That means that between 82% and 91% of political contributions come from the Oligarchs, the companies they control and millionaires (often through the Political Action Committees [PACs] they control). The quid pro quo for political contributions is influence on our politicians. The results of this influence are in plain sight—huge tax breaks for the wealthy, business-friendly laws and regulations, an unbalanced U.S. Supreme Court, union suppression and an ever-widening income-and-wealth gap.

My recommendation is to change the Federal Election Laws and pass legislation to neutralize the Citizens United decision to make it illegal for corporations to spend unlimited amounts on campaigns. Also, PACs need to be open about their funding. We should set a low limit on the amount anyone (including corporations) can contribute to a candidate—say $400. This would not only stop the outsized influence enjoyed by the wealthy but also return campaign spending to reasonable levels. Better yet, let's finally move to government-financed elections.

Absent these changes, PACs should be formed so the 95% of Americans whose voices are not currently being heard can pool their contributions. I suggest we call it the ***American Contribution Political Action Committee*** (ACPAC). There are around 209-million people in the U.S. 18-years of age and older. The adults who make less than $100,000 per year total approximately 199-million. If every adult who makes less than $100,000 per year contributed $50 per election cycle to the ACPAC, it would be able to deploy $10-billion in campaign contributions in every cycle.

To put that into perspective, in the 2020 election cycle, presidential candidates, congressional candidates, party committees and PACs of both parties raised and spent around $14-billion. With a war chest of $10-billion, the ACPAC can secure (buy) influence at least equal to that of the Oligarchs. If the 199-million adults donated $100 per election cycle to the ACPAC, it would have $20-billion in available campaign contributions. Couple that war chest with 199-million votes and you have a very powerful force to ensure that the interests of most Americans are being served—not just 5%.

Unlimited Dollars: The American dollar is a fiat currency (inconvertible paper money made legal tender by a government decree). The U.S. dollar is legal tender for making financial transactions. It must be accepted if offered in payment for goods, services and debt. Its value is backed by the full faith and credit of the U.S. government. The government promises to be good for it. The U.S. Federal Bank (the Fed) is responsible for maintaining the supply of U.S. dollars.

According to the U.S. Federal Reserve System's Website, the "Federal Reserve Act of 1913 established the Federal Reserve System as the central bank of the United States to provide the nation with a safer, more flexible, and more stable monetary and financial system. The law sets out the purposes, structure, and functions of the System as well as outlines aspects of its operations and accountability. *Congress has the power to amend the Federal Reserve Act* (emphasis mine), *which it has done several times over the years."* For example, in 1977 Congress mandated the Fed to also "promote effectively the goals of maximum employment, stable prices and moderate long-term interest rates."

According to the U.S. Federal Reserve Bank (Fed), in September 2020 the total U.S. currency in circulation was a little over $2-trillion. One-hundred years earlier (September 1920) there was $5.3-billion in circulation. At the turn of the 21st Century, $570-billion was in circulation. A graph of this data shows that the amount of currency in circulation grew relatively slowly from 1920 to 1980—$5.3-billion to $136-billion. After 1980, the graph turns sharply upward to reach the $2-trillion level in 2020. The population of the U.S. in 1920 was 160-million. In 2020, it is 331-million. That means that in 1920 there was $33 in circulation for every American. Today, over $6,400 is in circulation for every American.

Where do all these dollars come from? They are created by the Fed out of thin air in the form of computer bytes. The Fed creates these dollars through open market operations by purchasing U.S.-government securities in the market using new money it has "created" or by "creating" bank reserves issued to commercial banks. The Fed is responsible for creating and destroying billions of U.S. dollars every day.

The Fed is also responsible for printing new dollar bills. However, the modern Federal Reserve no longer simply runs new paper bills off a printing press. Some physical bill printing does still occur (with the help of the U.S. Department of the Treasury), but most of the American money supply is digitally debited and credited to the Federal Government and the major banks.

It is estimated that approximately 92% of all U.S. dollars issued by the government are in digital form, not in printed bills. By now, we're all familiar with this reality. Most of us have relatively few printed dollars in our pockets or stuffed under our mattresses. Our money is stored on one-or-more servers in digital form. This is also true of everyone's net worth. We use these "digital dollars" to make purchases, pay our bills and make investments.

For example, I currently pay all my routine bills via electronic transfers of one kind or another. When I use my credit cards, the money I'm spending is electronically transferred from my credit-card bank to the vendor. I electronically transfer money from my checking account to my credit-card bank when I pay my credit-card bill. Money is deposited into my checking account electronically from the U.S. government (retirement) and by direct deposits from other sources. No printed dollars are involved in these transactions.

The Fed's <u>Federal Open Market Committee</u> (FOMC) meets regularly to assess the U.S. money supply and general economic condition of the country. The FOMC consists of 12 members—the 7 members of the Board of Governors of the Federal Reserve System, the president of the Federal Reserve Bank of New York and 4 of the remaining 11 Reserve Bank presidents. The FOMC holds 8 regularly scheduled meetings each year to determine monetary policies. These policies influence the availability and cost of money and credit to help promote national economic goals. The Federal Reserve Act of 1913 gave the Federal Reserve responsibility for setting monetary policy.

If it is determined that new money needs to be created, then the Fed targets a certain level of money injection and institutes a corresponding policy. That money could come from Fed <u>Open Market Operations</u> (OMO) where it buys and sells U.S.-government <u>Treasury Bonds</u> (T-bonds). So, if the Fed wants to inject $2-trillion into the economy, it can simply create the money (bytes) to buy $2-trillion worth of T-bonds in the market.

The Federal Government offers T-bonds, <u>Treasury Bills</u> and <u>Treasury Notes</u> to investors like the Fed and others as fixed-income securities. It can use the profits from selling the government bonds to fund its operations (like the *American Contribution Administration* and the *American Cornucopia Fund*). For investors, these investment vehicles offer safety and a predictable profit, but no opportunity for spectacular gains.

The Cornucopia Proposals call for the *American Contribution Administration* (ACA) to be funded by the *American Cornucopia Fund* (ACF), and that the

ACF be funded directly by dollars created by the Fed. The Fed could produce these dollars as described above and deposit them (in digital form) directly into the ACF account for use by the ACA. Or, the Fed could use its traditional method of buying T-Bonds.

The ACA's budget would be approved every 5-years by the U.S. Congress. This 5-year budget provides increased security and consistency for the ACA's budget requirements. Since the ACA's annual expenditures will be considerable, a 5-year funding plan will assist the Fed in developing its inflation-control plans.

My calculations indicate that the *American Contribution Administration* (ACA) will require something like $50-trillion dollars a year to fund its operations—administration, *the American Contribution Corp* (ACC), the *American Contributor Trust Fund* (ACTF), the *American Common Good Fund* (ACGF) and other ACA programs.

At first blush, $50-trillion seems like pie-in-the-sky thinking. After all, the U.S. GDP was around $22-trillion per year before the pandemic. If we add the $50-trillion ACA spending to the U.S. GDP, our economy will expand to around $72-trillion a year. That level of economic activity will make the rich richer, ensure the physical and economic security of the 95% of Americans who are now experiencing a standard of living that is far below where it could be, and it will maintain the U.S. as the world's largest economy. And, it will replace untold trillions in spending for welfare, education, healthcare, etc.

But, what about inflation? Isn't it common knowledge that if a government starts "printing money" (In this case, in digital form.), hyperinflation will soon follow? In my opinion, not necessarily.

The money that was given to the Oligarchs in the Emergency Economic Stabilization Act of 2008 totaled over $700-billion. The 2020 Coronaviris Bailout has been over $2-trillion as of November 2020. It is expected that at least an additional $10-trillion will be required before the economic effects of the pandemic can be reversed.

These "bailouts" or "economic-stimulus packages" where funded by the Fed by creating new money that was injected into the U.S. economy in several ways. As the 2008 and 2020 injections of new money into the economy were taking place, Congress granted huge tax cuts to the rich that will total in the trillions-of-dollars. The tax cuts significantly unbalanced the federal budget.

The money needed to cover the budget shortfalls was and will be created by the Fed.

Over the past 12-years or so, around $3-trillion was "printed" by the Fed and injected into the economy through various means. However, the average annual rate of inflation has been 1.7% over this period. This is below the Fed's target inflation rate of 2%. Obviously, the Fed is capable of injecting new money into the economy without causing hyperinflation. I know that there is a big difference between $3-trillion and $50-trillion, but will creating $50-trillion and injecting it into the economy through the *American Cornucopia Fund* (ACF) by itself cause hyperinflation?

Wikipedia defines hyperinflation as a "very high and typically accelerating rate of inflation". Inflation is typically termed "hyperinflation" if the rate of inflation exceeds 50% per month. It quickly erodes the real value of the local currency as the prices of all goods increase. Wikipedia lists 18 instances of hyperinflation since the 3rd Century.

After reviewing these 18 instances of hyperinflation, it appears to me that several factors must be present to precipitate it. The increase in an economy's money supply through the "printing" of money is only one of them. Usually, societal unrest, war or other major upsets to a country's fiscal situation are present when hyperinflation occurs. It also has a lot to do with an unbalance in the demand-supply equation. And, hyperinflation can occur when there is a significant increase in the money supply that is not matched by economic growth.

If *The Cornucopia Proposals* are adopted, there will be a rapid increase in economic growth that will occur in tandem with the increase in the money supply. And, I believe that we can develop big-data systems that will enable us to keep the demand-supply equation in equilibrium.

Given the Fed's track record on injecting new money into the economy while keeping inflation low, I'm confident that the Fed, Congress and the *American Contribution Administration* (ACA) can come up with the policies, procedures and practices that can "meter" the introduction of new money into the economy while controlling the factors that may lead to hyperinflation. In fact, the Fed was mandated by Congress in the Federal Reserve Act of 1913 to manage America's money supply while controlling inflation and striving for full employment. *The Cornucopia Proposals* provides an innovative way for the Fed to fulfill these sometimes-conflicting mandates.

The full-employment mandate is going to become more difficult for the Fed to manage as more Americans are displaced from the workforce by consolidation, artificial intelligence, robotics and global competition. These displacements are becoming more-and-more common. If we don't adopt *The Cornucopia Proposals*, or some other viable strategy, the risk of having a significant portion of the U.S. workforce on the poverty rolls will be far greater than the risk of creating hyperinflation.

In summary:

1. The King James version of the Christian Bible (1 Timothy, 6:10) states "for the love of money is the root of all evil". I'm sure you can think of many examples of money, and/or the pursuit thereof, corrupting Americans to the point that they are willing (eager?) to commit what most of us consider to be evil deeds to gain and maintain ascendancy over the rest of us.

   However, money is also at the root of modern-day happiness. In our society, everyone requires money to purchase the goods and services they need for their survival and their practice of happiness. I think we can all agree that a sufficient supply of money is required to satisfy our Physiological and Safety Needs. It is also needed to provide us with many of the resources required to satisfy our Social, Esteem and Self-Actualization Needs (see "Maslow's Hierarchy of Needs" in Chapter 3). And, as we've already seen, if we can satisfy the needs of Maslow's Hierarchy, we can be happy.

2. Based on my experiences, observations and calculations, I believe that a net-annual-personal income of $100,000 is required to enable adult Americans to climb Maslow's pyramid to happiness.

3. America is facing several challenges that may well determine the fate of the human race (inequality, poverty, climate-change, automation, etc.). We need to focus as much brain power as possible on meeting these challenges. Hiring Americans to work on solving these problems, and paying them $100,000 a year to do so, will make it more likely that we make it to the other side of the looming abys that threatens to put the progress we've made over the millennia into reverse gear.

4. The median individual income in the U.S. in 2019 was $40,100. By increasing the annual individual income to $100,000 for 95% of our

citizens, the American economy will get a significant boost, the rich will get richer and the rest of us will have an adequate secure basic income that will satisfy our needs.

5. America has been using fiat money since the Emergency Banking Act of 1933 was enacted. The Federal Reserve Bank, established in 1913 with the enactment of the Federal Reserve Act has the power to "create" as much money as it sees fit. Therefore, there is an unlimited supply of money to fund *The Cornucopia Proposals*. No tax dollars required.

6. In fact, the Fed can create enough money to fund federal-, state- and local-government budgets too. So, we can eliminate federal, state and local taxes and replace the tax revenues with money from the *American Cornucopia Fund*. This should appeal to the Oligarchs and everyone else in the country. Nobody likes to pay taxes!

7. The biggest concern with the Fed injecting new money into the economy is hyperinflation. I believe the country can manage the increase in the money supply with innovative policies, procedures and practices that balance supply with demand, keep inflation low and maximize the power of the human resources that America is blessed with.

Now that we've determined how we're going to get to where we want to go, let's look at the pros and cons of adopting *The Cornucopia Proposals*:

Pros:

1. A real opportunity for all Americans to climb Maslow's Pyramid, to achieve lasting happiness and to live the American Dream.

2. A guaranteed job with a guaranteed livable income for every adult American who joins the *American Contribution Corps*.

3. A guaranteed livable retirement income for every *American Contribution Corps* member when they choose to retire at age 70 or older.

4. Universal, government-paid healthcare for every *American Contribution Corps* member who wants it.

5. Universal, government-paid education and training for every *American Contribution Corps* member.

6. The elimination of poverty in America with the consequent savings for the Treasury with the elimination of current poverty programs.

7. A significant reduction in violent crimes.

8. Rapid and significant growth of the American economy. The rich will get richer and the poor and middle class will prosper too.

9. American research and development will accelerate.

10. America's most-pressing societal problems will get solved when tens-of-millions of Americans are working on solving them.

11. The American workforce will be much-more productive.

12. The work-life balance of most Americans will be the best in the world.

13. Long-term growth and prosperity, rather than short-term profits, will become America's guiding light.

14. Americans will more-equally enjoy their unalienable rights of Life, Liberty and the pursuit of Happiness.

15. The American government will more-accurately represent the needs and desires of every American.

16. American businesses will enjoy significantly increased profits and lower risk with a government-paid-for workforce and the shedding of employee-benefit and training costs.

17. The shifting of the source of funds for running local, state and federal government operations to the *American Cornucopia Fund* (ACF) will eliminate the need for income, real-estate and sales taxes. This will also stabilize government at all levels and ensure proper infrastructure improvements.

18. A solution for the affordable-housing problem—everyone will be able to afford decent housing.

19. A solution for the child-care crisis. When needed, it will be paid for by the *American Contribution Corps*. Child-care-industry workers will be readily available at no cost to the Child-care facilities through the Corp.

20. Non-governmental, non-profit organizations will have the money and people power they need to increase the effectiveness and reach of their programs that are focused on increasing the common good.

21. The American workforce will be continually educated and trained to the level required by the economy.

22. The stability of family life will be significantly enhanced. This will produce more-stable, clear-thinking and productive Americans.

23. The *American Contribution Corps* code-of-conduct and ongoing training programs will align most Americans to a standardized matrix of norms, practices, ethics and behavior that will enhance the common good.

24. The *American Contribution Corps* basic pay of $100,000 per year will provide every Corps member with the means to satisfy his/her Physiological and Safety Needs as well as the basis for self-respect, self-esteem and self-actualization.

25. The American-capitalism system will be maintained with a few upgrades to it.

26. The Oligarchs will remain in power.

27. No American will experience a reduction in social status. All boats will rise.

Cons:

1. A risk of hyperinflation.

2. Some profit streams will be shifted from one sector of the economy to others.

3. A risk that the rate of depletion of our national resources will be increased by higher consumption.

4. A risk that climate change may be accelerated by increased consumption.

5. The Oligarchs will have to loosen their grip on the capitalism pendulum just a little and let it start to swing back towards stakeholder capitalism just a bit.

6. The risk that Congress will be deadlocked due to partisan politics and won't pass the *American Contribution Act of 2021*.

Q&A:

The following questions have been asked about *The Cornucopia Proposals* by the people I have talked with about them. I humbly offer my answers to those questions.

1. **What if I can't or don't want to devote 20-hours per week to the American Contribution Corps?** *The 20-hours per week is a full-time commitment. You can work a minimum of 10-hours per week for a $50,000 annual salary plus benefits.*

2. **Will the growth enabled by the adoption of *The Cornucopia Proposals* deplete our available natural resources at an even higher rate than we are now?** *Initially, yes. But, as the American Contribution Corps (ACC) members who are assigned to the American Contribution Administration (ACA) task forces that are working on solving our resource and environmental problems, I'm confident they will find solutions that reduce our consumption levels, increase recycling and identify how to do more with less. In the early*

1980s, one of my mentors, R. Buckminster (Bucky) Fuller, pointed out to me that Americans have been learning how to do more with less for quite some time now. It is reasonable, I believe, to assume this trend will continue.

3. **How will the *Cornucopia Proposals* effect climate change?** *The American Contribution Administration (ACA) task forces that will be working on solving our climate-change problem will, I'm convinced, come up with viable plans to mitigate this existential risk. The resources needed—brainpower and money—to solve this problem will be readily available.*

4. **How will *The Cornucopia Proposals* effect work-life balance?** *American's work-life balance will become one of the best on the planet. Worker angst about job security, healthcare, job mobility, equality of pay, child care, retirement and fair treatment at work will be all but eliminated.*

5. **How will *The Cornucopia Proposals* effect the happiness of all Americans?** *By providing every adult American with the resources they need—time, money, opportunity and guidance—to climb Maslow's Pyramid, most Americans, on average, will experience "happiness". The Founders' vision of Life, Liberty and the pursuit (practice) of happiness will be realized.*

6. **How will we pay for *The Cornucopia Proposals*?** *The money will come from the American Cornucopia Fund (ACF). The ACF will be funded by the Fed by creating new "money".*

7. **Why pay *American Contribution Corps* members $100,000 per year when other minimum-guaranteed-income programs have provided much less?** *Several minimum-guaranteed-income and basic-income pilot programs have been tested around the world including in America. They have for the most part (when coupled with other social-welfare programs) worked well in alleviating the worst poverty. However, the monthly payments have been only a few hundred dollars. This is grossly insufficient to provide Americans with the resources they need to climb Maslow's Pyramid.*

The primary goal of these pilot programs has been a reduction in poverty. The primary goal of The Cornucopia Proposals is to make the American dream truly possible for every American.

8. **If I like my job, can I join the Corps for the security it offers and still work for the company I'm working for now?** *Yes. If the company you are now working for submits a personnel-support request and names you in the request, you will be offered the job before other Corps members.*

   If the request is approved, you will be obligated to work for that employer for 20-hours per week. If the employer wants you to work more than that, you and the employer will negotiate your fee for the extra work.

9. **Who is going to do the dirty work?** *In answering this question, I like to use sanitation workers as an example of how it will work. But, the answer also applies to most of the jobs that "no one wants to do". Part of every sanitation worker's job will be to come up with ways to reduce the number of sanitation-worker hours that are required to pick up America's trash.*

   For example, when I was a kid in the 1950s, garbage trucks were manned by 3 sanitation workers. Today, they are generally manned by 1 person. This reduction was enabled by rather-simple technology. Somebody just had to think of it.

   Another answer to this question is that the sanitation workforce will be made up of current sanitation workers who are willing to work 20-hours per week for $100,000 per year. Of course, not every current sanitation worker will want to remain on the job when they have other viable options.

   Some people will decide to meet their 20-hour-per-week American Contribution Corps (ACC) work obligation by driving a garbage truck. The maximum-required tour of duty as a sanitation worker will be 6-months. If there are not enough volunteers, workers will be drafted from among Corps members who are between the ages of 18 and 30 who are not considered to be essential in the jobs they are in or who are not assigned to other ACC jobs.

10. **If I'm comfortable with my current situation regarding income, healthcare, etc., do I have to join the American Contribution Corps?** *No. Membership in the Corps is strictly voluntary. However, if you're not an active or retired Corp member, you will not receive*

the benefits enjoyed by being a member.

11. **Can I join the Corps and work from home?** *Yes. If the job you want can be done remotely, you have the option of working from home.*

12. **How can the adoption of *The Cornucopia Proposals* eliminate taxes?** *Throughout history, the rich, poor and virtually everyone in between has complained about having to pay taxes. This is especially true for the rich. In general, they believe that the money that flows into their bank accounts is theirs and they don't have to share it with anyone else—including their neighbors even if their neighbors are starving.*

    Over the years, more-or-less continuous attempts at convincing the rich to "pay their fair share" have fallen on deaf ears. In America today, the Oligarchs and their big corporations pay little-to-no U.S. taxes. But, they are under constant pressure from their neighbors to relax their tight fists. And the 95% of Americans who are not "rich" are annoyed at having their already inadequate wages reduced by paying taxes. And, no one enjoys having to file tax returns every year.

    Adoption of The Cornucopia Proposals *will make both the 5% and the 95% happy by eliminating all taxes that fund local, state and federal governments. Operations for all levels of government will be funded by the American Cornucopia Fund with "dollars" that are created by the Fed rather than by tax revenues.*

13. **Are we going to put tax accountants out of business?** *Yes. Since there will be no more local, state or federal income taxes, the income-tax-preparation industry will no longer be needed. However, the accountants who make a living by preparing individual and corporate tax returns will be needed in other sectors of the economy as it grows rapidly and businesses expand. And, those accountants who don't want to transition to another area of accountancy will have the opportunity to join the American Contribution Corps and pursue any career, passion or interest they want.*

14. **Won't the national debt become ruinous if *The Cornucopia Proposals* are adopted?** *Let's define the national debt as the total amount of money that is deposited in the American Cornucopia Fund*

(ACF) by the Fed over time plus accrued interest. And let's assume the Fed purchases T-Bonds to inject the new money into federal-government coffers. In this case, the government would be paying the interest on the T-Bonds with new money that is being created by the Fed. And, the government would have to return the principal amount of the bonds to the Fed at maturity. The payoffs on the bonds would also come from new money created by the Fed and then transferred to the federal government through the sale of new T-Bonds. The debt payoff would flow back into Fed coffers.

Of course, this process will evolve into a spiral of increasing debt. But, what if the Fed periodically forgave the repayment of the debt? After all, the Fed doesn't need to recover the principal and interest because it doesn't have to "balance its books" or make a profit on the T-Bonds it purchases from the government.

15. **Can we really make *The Cornucopia Proposals* happen?** *The proposals will be adopted if most of the 199-million American adults who are making less than $100,000 per year make the effort to open-mindedly understand the implications of adopting the proposals, and if they take action to make the American Contribution Act of 2021 a reality. If they do, their representatives in Congress will be compelled to pass the legislation. And, it will help immensely if the Oligarchs see the wisdom in agreeing the proposals are good for them as well as other Americans.*

The process by which we can enable the changes in thinking that are required is, in my opinion, essentially a culture-change effort. It can take a very long time for a culture to change, or it can change rather quickly. I witnessed this first hand in the early 1980s when I led a team that enabled rapid culture change (90-days) in several airline-employee groups in response to the changes that were manifested by airline deregulation. I believe the methods we used then, augmented by new media techniques, can be used to turn things around quickly with a modest resource requirement.

16. **What makes you think the Oligarchs will go along with *The Cornucopia Proposals?*** *Veblen Thorstein in his landmark 1899 book "The Theory of the Leisure Class: An Economic Study of Institutions" pointed out that the "rich" are addicted to what he called "conspicuous consumption" as a function of social class. It is derived from social stratification and the division of labor.*

Conspicuous consumption is a competitive sport. It eschews "keeping up with the Jones'" and embraces "mine's bigger than yours" thinking. If you are a competitor in this sport, you must continue to make more-and-more money to buy bigger-and-better things with which to display your social status.

The Cornucopia Proposals do not threaten the Oligarchs enjoyment of conspicuous consumption in any way. They will still have so much more than the most Americans that their social status will not be threatened. And, the elimination of income taxes will allow them to keep what they have just like they want to.

Also, although it is generally believed the king-serf model of society has been relegated to the past, the Oligarchs still must fear a violent uprising by the 95% of Americans who are becoming increasingly frustrated and militant about their situation if things are allowed to get too bad. If I was an Oligarch, my sleep would be troubled by dreams of peasants storming the gates of my castle with pitchforks and torches in hand. By allowing The Cornucopia Proposals to be adopted, the Oligarchs will be able to sleep more soundly. And, they will benefit immensely from the goodwill that will be generated by their munificence.

About the only negative I see for the Oligarchs in adopting The Cornucopia Proposals is the loss of interest income from government bonds if all government operations are funded by the American Cornucopia Fund (ACF) rather than by government borrowing from individuals and financial institutions. However, I think this could be rectified by allowing the Oligarchs to purchase a reasonable amount of bonds.

17. **Won't the 74-*million* Trump voters oppose the proposals?**
Probably initially. Research shows that the people who voted for Trump have a strong orientation towards authoritarianism, social dominance and prejudice and they have little interaction with people of other races. They believe they have been unfairly deprived of the social rewards they are entitled to and others have undeservedly done better in life than them.

Due to their devotion to Trump, they will probably not get onboard with the proposals unless Trump endorses them. However, the famous Scottish economist and philosopher Adam Smith (1723 – 1790) believed that people will always make the decision that brings the greatest reward at the lowest cost. This theory is at the heart of capitalism and a market economy. Since Trump voters are believers in the market, they may act as Smith predicted and see that the manifold benefits that will accrue to them if The Cornucopia Proposals are adopted are the reward they've been seeking and that they believe they deserve. And, they can enjoy the benefits of the proposals at a very-low cost to them. After all, the proposals will be funded through the American Cornucopia Fund, *not their tax dollars.*

And, they won't have to feel jealous of others, especially minorities, who are successful because the Trump voters will have the same support and opportunities as everyone. And, they can quit worrying about the poor getting "handouts" because the poor will no longer be so—they'll all be working at jobs that provide them with a livable income.

Even if Trump voters never get onboard with The Cornucopia Proposals, *if the rest of us are organized and active in advocating for the proposals, the majority will rule. Remember there are 125-million Americans of voting age who did not vote for Trump.*

18. **Don't *The Cornucopia Proposals* sound too good to be true?** *They should sound very good to every American. But "too good to be true"? I'm sure some of the American colonists thought the Declaration of Independence and Constitution sounded too good to be true when they first heard about them. But, look what happened. And, of course, they won't become true unless we decide to make them true.*

Thank you for taking your time to read and think about *The Cornucopia Proposals*. I trust that your journey was smooth and that my logic is reasonable to you.

It took me several years of research and thinking before I came to the conclusions I've reached and presented to you. I probably would have just kept on thinking about them for several more years before writing this book if the Covid-19 pandemic hadn't invaded my well-ordered and busy life. So, maybe there's a silver lining in the current turmoil.

Because of the research I've done, I have changed my thinking about the American economy being a zero-sum game. I have come to realize that it is, in reality, a cornucopia that can supply the American people with the resources they need to be able to enjoy their unalienable rights of Life, Liberty and the pursuit of Happiness.

If you now believe as I do, and if other of Americans also come to think like us about *The Cornucopia Proposals*, I am all but certain the *American Contribution Act of 2021*, or something like it, will become a reality.

Part of the reason I believe that is because the culture-change projects I worked on in the 1980s garnered from 85% to 96% support for the changes that needed to be made. Also, my experiences have shown me that if you believe you can achieve a goal, you're half-way there.

I also think the time is right for *The Cornucopia Proposals*. Recent polls indicate 70% of Americans are for guaranteed jobs. Millions of Americans have been in the streets for the past several months marching for equal treatment under the law and in society. Tens-of-millions of Americans are now out of work and their prospects for returning to work soon don't look good.

The 2020 election cycle has highlighted the unemployment issue and lifted the curtain on the impact artificial intelligence, robotics and automation will have on Americans in the future. And, the Covid-19 pandemic and Trump's presidency have provided us with the impetus to open our minds and to think in different ways about how we want our country to treat its people.

My experience as an entrepreneur provides me with optimism about our chances for organizing and implementing the changes that will be needed to make *The Cornucopia Proposals* a reality. Entrepreneurism, after all, is the process of establishing a new, sustainable entity in a highly uncertain environment.

I believe there are more than enough smart entrepreneurs, economists, political scientists and others in America who, if they believe, can flesh out the details of *The Cornucopia Proposals*. And, if enough Americans believe in them and take action to make them a reality, I think there is a very good chance they will become the law of the land.

So, please let me know what you think about *The Cornucopia Proposals*. Just drop me a line at dkoch@cornucopiaproposals.org. And, please share *The Cornucopia Proposals* with your family, friends, associates and political representatives.

Above all, contribute to making *The Cornucopia Proposals* a reality in every way you can. I firmly believe that if the proposals are adopted, America will be a much better place to live for us, our children, our grandchildren and for many generations to come.

We have the opportunity and obligation at this unique point in history to significantly and positively change the course of the future. That kind of opportunity comes along all to infrequently. Let's not miss it.

-End-